THE EVERYTHI

PRACTICE INTERVIEW BOOK

Dear Reader,

Interviews are difficult. I know—I've been on both sides of the desk. I've interviewed job candidates and I've been interviewed for jobs myself. I can honestly think of many things that are a lot more fun and a lot less stressful. Of course, there's great deal of pressure on the job candidate. Anyone who has been interviewed for a job can attest to that. Your utmost desire is to make the interviewer see that you are the best person for the job. However, the interviewer faces pressure, too. She must make sure the candidate she selects is a good fit for the job and for the company in general.

In the more than a decade I've spent as the Guide to Career Planning on About.com (*http://careerplanning .about.com*) and in the years I spent before that managing a job information center in a public library, I've heard from many people who are incredibly anxious about going on job interviews. Mostly, job hunters want to know what questions to expect and how to answer them. I also get e-mails from people who have faced improper or illegal questions on a job interview. I made a point of including information on that topic in this book, as well as letting you know where to turn if you feel a prospective employer has discriminated against you.

To me, the best way to overcome the stress of job interviewing is to prepare for it as much as possible. I've included more than 300 questions in this book. Read them carefully and use them as a guide as you prepare for your own job interviews.

Good luck!

Dawn Rosenberg McKay

THE

EVERYTHING

Series

These handy, accessible books give you all you need to tackle a difficult project, gain a new hobby, or even brush up on something you learned back in school but have since forgotten. You can choose to read from cover to cover or just pick out information from our four useful boxes.

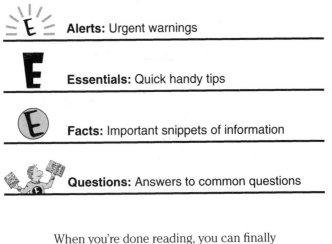

Alerts: Urgent warnings

Essentials: Quick handy tips

Facts: Important snippets of information

Questions: Answers to common questions

When you're done reading, you can finally say you know **EVERYTHING**®!

PUBLISHER Karen Cooper

DIRECTOR OF ACQUISITIONS AND INNOVATION Paula Munier

MANAGING EDITOR, EVERYTHING SERIES Lisa Laing

COPY CHIEF Casey Ebert

ACQUISITIONS EDITOR Lisa Laing

DEVELOPMENT EDITOR Elizabeth Kassab

EDITORIAL ASSISTANT Hillary Thompson

Visit the entire Everything® series at *www.everything.com*

THE
EVERYTHING®
PRACTICE INTERVIEW BOOK

2ND EDITION

Make the best impression—
and get the job you want!

Dawn Rosenberg McKay

Avon, Massachusetts

To Dean, Rebec
and love, everyt

An Everything® Series Book.
Everything® and everything.com® are registered
trademarks of F+W Media, Inc.

Published by Adams Media, a division of F+W Media, Inc.
57 Littlefield Street, Avon, MA 02322 U.S.A.
www.adamsmedia.com

ISBN 10: 1-60550-050-X
ISBN 13: 978-1-60550-050-8

Printed in the United States of America.

J I H G F E D C B A

Library of Congress Cataloging-in-Publication Data
is available from the publisher.

This book is available at quantity discounts for bulk purchases.
For information, please call 1-800-289-0963.

Contents

Top Ten Things Not to Say on a Job Interview | **viii**

Introduction | **ix**

CHAPTER 1: PREPARING FOR THE INTERVIEW | **1**

Understanding Job Interviews | **1**

Learning about Yourself | **5**

Learning about Your Prospective Employer | **7**

Take Time to Rehearse | **16**

Access Your Network | **17**

Dealing with Anxiety | **18**

What to Do about Low Confidence | **19**

The Night Before and Morning of the Interview | **20**

CHAPTER 2: FIRST IMPRESSIONS COUNT | **22**

What to Wear to the Interview | **22**

What to Bring to the Interview | **27**

Getting to the Interview on Time | **28**

Arriving for Your Appointment | **29**

The Interview Begins | **29**

Body Language | **31**

Making Your Exit | **35**

Interviewing over a Meal | **36**

Interviewing in a Foreign Country | **38**

CHAPTER 3: REVEALING YOUR PERSONALITY | **40**

Why the Personal Questions? | **40**

Questions and Answers | **42**

CHAPTER 4: DISCUSSING YOUR SKILLS AND ABILITIES | **57**
Hard Skills Versus Soft Skills | **57**
Skills You Haven't Used Professionally | **59**
Questions and Answers | **60**

CHAPTER 5: HIGHLIGHTING YOUR ACCOMPLISHMENTS | **75**
Listing Your Accomplishments | **75**
Discussing Your Accomplishments | **76**
Questions and Answers | **77**

CHAPTER 6: QUESTIONS ABOUT YOUR EDUCATION | **93**
How You Spent Your College Years | **93**
Questions and Answers | **95**

CHAPTER 7: DISCUSSING YOUR WORK HISTORY | **111**
How to Present Your Past | **111**
Questions and Answers | **113**

CHAPTER 8: YOUR INTERPERSONAL SKILLS | **128**
An Employee Balancing Act | **128**
How Do You Resolve Conflicts? | **129**
Questions and Answers | **130**

CHAPTER 9: DID YOU DO YOUR HOMEWORK? | **147**
Proving Your Knowledge | **147**
Highlight Skills That Fit the Company | **148**
Questions and Answers | **149**

CHAPTER 10: WHAT WOULD YOU DO IF YOU WERE HIRED? | **165**
What You Can Bring to the Company | **165**
What the Company Expects of You | **166**
Questions and Answers | **168**

Chapter 11: Difficult or Embarrassing Questions | **183**
I Hope They Don't Ask Me That | **183**
How to Answer Difficult Questions | **184**
Questions and Answers | **186**

Chapter 12: Dealing with Illegal Questions | **202**
Laws That Protect You from Discrimination | **202**
What Questions Are Illegal? | **206**
Questions and Answers | **207**

Chapter 13: Behavioral Interviews | **222**
Behavioral Interviews: The Basics | **222**
How to Answer Behavioral Questions | **224**
Questions and Answers | **225**

Chapter 14: Do You Have Any Questions? | **244**
Asking Questions Is a Must | **244**
Preparing Your Questions | **246**
Questions You *Should* Ask and Questions You *Should Not* Ask | **246**

Chapter 15: What to Do after the Interview | **257**
Thank-You Letters | **257**
What to Do If You Don't Want the Job | **266**
Waiting for a Decision | **269**
The Job Offer—Finally | **270**

Appendix A: Resources | **272**

Appendix B: Glossary | **281**

Index | **288**

Top Ten Things Not to Say
on a Job Interview

1. That suit looks expensive! How much money do you make, anyway?
2. What will my salary be? My rent is very high!
3. I've never heard of this company before. What type of business is this?
4. It wasn't my fault I got fired. My boss always had it in for me.
5. I quit my job because my coworkers were all idiots. I didn't like working with any of them.
6. How much time do you give for maternity leave?
7. How much vacation time would I have? I need a lot of time off for traveling.
8. If someone files a sexual harassment charge against me, you'll have my back, right?
9. This isn't exactly what I want to be doing but let's see what happens.
10. I'll really need to have my own office. I don't like working with other people.

Introduction

WOULDN'T IT BE NICE if you could send out your resume for a position you're qualified for and simply be offered a job? After all, everything about you is right there on your resume, isn't it? You should know—you put it there yourself.

But, no, everything about you is not on your resume. Think of your resume as a pencil sketch of who you really are. There is no dimension to it. It has no color and no expression. Basically, it's pretty flat. Not at all like you; you are multifaceted. You've made choices throughout your career. You've reached certain goals and celebrated many accomplishments. You should have a chance to talk about all of that, because those details are what will make an employer want to hire you.

The job interview is your chance to show your prospective employer who you really are and what you can bring to the position. By asking you questions, a prospective employer can learn all about you and why you made the choices you made. He can discover what motivates you and what makes you proud. The interviewer can find out how you will fit in with his company. Will you get along with other employees? Will you make important contributions to his organization?

There is a lot to accomplish during the job interview. It is perhaps the most important part of the entire job search process. It is also the most difficult part of the entire job search process. It's not like the resume you spent months poring over. You can edit your resume again and again until it lists the most important things about your career and uses the most effective wording to highlight your skills. However, a job interview usually takes place in less than an hour. When you say something, there's no delete key. If you forget to say something, the moment may have already passed by the time you realize it.

That is why it is so very important that you prepare well for the job interview. You won't have another chance to get it right, at least not with the same employer. The more comfortable you are with the entire process of interviewing, the more relaxed you will be when it comes time for the interview, and the better the interview will be.

This book will guide you through the entire job interview process. The first two chapters cover everything you need to do before the interview takes place. Discover what you need to do to prepare for a job interview. Learn how to research a prospective employer so you can intelligently ask and answer questions during your interview. Find out how to dress for an interview. Learn about interviewing in another country.

Next up are twelve chapters that are packed full of sample job interview questions. For each question there is a great answer, an explanation of why you should give that answer, and then an answer you should never give and the reason why. As you go through the questions, think of how you would answer each one, using your own unique traits, experiences, and educational background.

The final chapter deals with the aftermath of the job interview. Find out what you need to do to follow up on a job interview. Is a thank-you letter really necessary? Of course, the whole purpose of this entire process is to get a job offer. Find out how to negotiate, accept, or reject one. By the time you're finished with this book, you'll be able to take on even the toughest interview.

Chapter 1

Preparing for the Interview

MANY PEOPLE FOLLOW a certain routine when they are job hunting. They send copies of their resumes to prospective employers and follow that with weeks of sitting around waiting to be called back. You should let your competition follow that routine—you can make much better use of your time! By preparing for a job interview in advance, you will increase your chances of getting hired when you finally do get that call.

Understanding Job Interviews

Before you begin interviewing, you must make sure you have a good understanding of what interviews are all about. You should know about the interview process, the different types of interviews, and what employers are trying to learn about you from an interview. Becoming more knowledgeable about what to expect will help you demystify the entire interview process. This in turn will allow you to feel more confident when you are on a job interview. Remember, the more confident you feel, the more confident you will look to your potential boss.

Getting to Know You

Have you ever wondered what the point of a job interview is? The employer has your resume—can't she just look at it to see whether you have the necessary skills and experience? All she has to do is make a phone call or two to verify that information, right? While your resume is made up of information about your past experience, it doesn't give the employer a full picture of who you are. Your resume is only a summary of your skills, work experience, and educational background. With only your resume to rely on, the person interviewing you won't have any idea of the specific things about you that will set you apart from the other candidates.

Essential

Remember that the interview is your chance to expand upon the facts you listed on your resume. Rather than thinking of an interview as an inquisition, you should instead look at it as a wonderful opportunity to express your true self to your prospective employer.

After all, a resume is merely a piece of paper and you are so much more than that. An interviewer can't learn about someone's personality by looking at a resume. She can't discover how a candidate developed some of his skills or which accomplishments meant the most to him. The interviewer can't find out how the candidate reacts to change or adversity by reading his resume.

The only way an interviewer can learn any of those things about a job candidate is by talking to him and asking questions. This will allow the candidate to paint a picture of himself that is much more elaborate than what can fit on one sheet of paper.

Getting to Know Your Prospective Employer

Another purpose of a job interview is to help you to learn about the employer. You will discover things on a job interview that will allow you to make an informed decision about whether to accept or reject an offer should the employer make one. You will learn some things about the employer by asking questions. You will also learn things about the employer from the questions she asks you. For example, if the interviewer starts asking questions about working late or traveling, you can safely assume that these things will be part of your life if you get the job.

You may decide by the end of a job interview that this isn't really the job for you or that this company isn't one you want to work for. And that's okay. It is in everyone's best interests, both the employer's and yours, to make this determination before you accept a job offer and begin working.

The Interview Process

The interview process can go on for quite a while. First, you may be asked to come in for a screening interview. The screening interview is your first interview with a particular employer. In some cases it may even take place over the telephone. During a screening interview, the person interviewing you will usually be someone who works in the human resources department, and he will want to verify items that are on your resume, such as dates of employment and schooling.

If the person who completes your screening interview is satisfied, he will most likely set up a selection interview. While someone from human resources may interview you again at this point, it is also likely that a department manager will interview you. The department manager, in addition to making sure you have the desirable skills and background, will want to make sure you have the right personality for the position.

Following the first selection interview, the employer may ask you to come back for subsequent interviews. During these further interviews, the employer may want to introduce you to other people in the company to make sure you are the right choice. Remember, you are still in the interviewing phase, so be on your best behavior.

The employer may call back other candidates as she tries to narrow down her choices. Sometimes you will be the only candidate who is asked to return for more interviews. That usually is good news, but don't consider it a done deal until you actually have a job offer.

 **Question**

> **What should I discuss on a second interview?**
> Use this opportunity to bring up something that you didn't get to talk about during the initial interview. Be prepared with an example of a specific skill or achievement you didn't have a chance to highlight before. Remember to explain how the example shows you are a good candidate for the particular position you want.

Preparing to Answer Questions

You will be asked a variety of questions on a job interview. These questions will pertain to your skills and abilities, accomplishments, education, and work history. You will also be asked questions about your strengths and weaknesses, your interests and hobbies, and your likes and dislikes, all of which will allow the employer to learn about your personal traits or characteristics.

In Chapters 3 through 13 you will find questions you might encounter on a job interview. While answers (both good and bad) are given, they are only guidelines. You should try to figure out how *you* will answer those questions. While you should not go into a job interview with a memorized script, you should have an idea of how you will answer most questions that will come your way. Chapter 14 will give you ideas for the types of questions you should ask the interviewer. Use these questions in the same way—as a guideline you can adapt to your particular situation, the company with which you are interviewing, and the industry it is in.

Special Types of Interviews

At some point during your job search, you may have to participate in a group interview. In a group interview, several candidates are interviewed at one time. This type of interview allows those who are natural leaders to show themselves, and its purpose is often to find out who stands out from the crowd or emerges as a leader. If you aren't a leader, don't worry—not everyone can be one. The job may not be the right one for you. Trying to be someone you are not will only make things difficult down the line, when you or your employer discover you're not the right fit for the job after all.

If, when you walk into an interview, you find yourself sitting at a table opposite several people, don't be alarmed. You are about to take part in a panel interview. This type of interview is also known as a committee interview and is often used when a group of people must collectively decide who to hire. During a panel interview, each member of the panel will ask you questions. The best thing you can do in this situation is stay calm and answer the questions one at a time.

Essential

During a panel interview, several people may be firing questions off at once. Listen carefully, but if you don't hear the question, politely ask the person who asked it to repeat herself. When you answer questions during a panel interview, directly address the person who asked the question by making eye contact with her.

Learning about Yourself

Your goal on a job interview is to give the best answers you can possibly give. In order to do that there's someone you need to get to know—yourself. You probably worked hard at putting together a great resume that highlights your skills, accomplishments, and experience. This was time well spent, since a great resume will help you line up the right interview. There is, however, only so much you can get across in a resume. You need to uncover what is behind that basic outline so you can present it to the interviewer and show him what an excellent candidate you really are.

Be Specific

Be prepared to give detailed answers to job interview questions. The interviewer, for example, will ask you about your skills. You know what skills you have, but can you discuss how you acquired them? What if the interviewer asks you about your accomplishments? You've no doubt accomplished a lot at work, but can you recall specifics? You will need to use anecdotes that clearly back up any claims you've made on your resume or that you make during the interview, so it is imperative that you prepare some. Look back at some of your experiences and get ready to provide good examples of your strengths when the subject comes up.

Go Beyond the Resume

The interviewer will likely use your resume to guide him through the interview. Study your resume in order to become intimately familiar with each item you have listed on it. You must be prepared to talk about and elaborate on every item on it since a resume, by definition, is just a brief summary of your work history. To keep it succinct, you only provided the most pertinent of details about your experience.

On a job interview, by contrast, the interviewer expects you to elaborate. Sit down with a clean copy of your resume and a notebook in front of you. Look at each job you have listed on your resume and think about every single one carefully, one at a time. What do you remember about the job? Do you remember why you started working there and why you left? What was it like working there? Take notes so you can study them later.

 Fact

Interviewers generally expect more than yes or no answers to their questions. You must give details that clearly explain your answer. When an interviewer asks you to discuss a particular situation, be ready to give a specific answer and expand upon it with brief examples.

You should try to recall details about the job beyond what you put on your resume. Did your boss rely on you to perform certain duties because of a particular strength you possess? Can you recall times when you were invaluable to your employer?

Do you remember which job was your favorite (or least favorite)? Can you recall what you liked (or disliked) about each one? Think about some projects you worked on. What skills did you use in order to complete those projects? What obstacles did you have to overcome to complete them? Did you most often work on a team or did you usually work alone? Can you give examples of projects you worked on as part of a team and those you worked on independently?

⋛Ɛ⋚ Alert

Don't exaggerate on your resume. If the information on your resume isn't completely true, it will be impossible for you to discuss it during a job interview without continuing to exaggerate or lie. By the time you are done, if you have not been caught, you will have presented yourself as a totally different person than who you really are.

A solid resume will list your major accomplishments. Try to remember what effort you put into achieving each one. Did the accomplishment help you reach a goal? How did it benefit the employer? Were you in any way rewarded for your achievement, perhaps with a promotion? If you take the time to recall all this information before your interview, you don't have to worry about long silences as you try to remember the facts while the pressure is on.

Learning about Your Prospective Employer

Nineteenth-century essayist Ralph Waldo Emerson said, "There is no knowledge that is not power." Make this adage your mantra as you prepare for job interviews, especially if you are wondering whether it is worth your while to spend time researching a prospective employer. Be assured—the time and effort you spend gathering information about a company for which you want to work is a wise investment.

In the business world, corporations do research all the time. They want information about their clients and their competitors because it helps them compete more effectively in the marketplace. This is called competitive intelligence and companies dedicate significant amounts of money to it. While the benefit of doing this research can be measured in higher sales figures and, ultimately, increased profits, your commitment to researching prospective employers can result in your performing better on the job interview than your competitors do. An added benefit is that, when it comes time to entertain an offer from an employer, you will have data that will help you make an informed decision.

What Do You Need to Know?

Before you begin to think that researching prospective employers will be an enormous task, remember that, unless you're planning to write an extensive treatise on an employer, you don't need to know everything there is to know about it. You only need to know some basic information.

⚡ Alert

Companies often hire professional librarians to do their research. You won't have that luxury, so you are encouraged to learn how to perform this task on your own. You can, of course, visit your local public library or college library and receive assistance there. Librarians will acquaint you with the research tools they have available.

First, you want a company description. Find out what the company does, i.e., what products or services it sells, to whom it sells them, and in what industry the company operates. You may be interviewing for a sales job, but you should know whether you will be selling cosmetics to drugstores or tools to mechanics.

Look at the organizational structure of the company. Is it a subsidiary of another one or is it a parent company? If it is the latter, find out what companies are its subsidiaries. Learn about a company's key personnel. You don't have to find extensive biographies, but you should know names and a bit about top executives and those for whom you will be working, if you know who they are.

Having knowledge about a company's financial situation is important both for the interview and for deciding whether to accept an offer of employment. After all, wouldn't you rather go to work for a company that is in good financial health than one that is struggling? Determine whether the company is privately or publicly held. The course of your research will very much depend on the answer to that question.

You should also know some details about a company's history. Find out what year the company was founded and by whom. Learn what the company's mission was and is. Has the company changed its focus over the years? Find out if the company ever faced any difficulties and how it overcame them.

Essential

If you have been away from your career for an extended period of time, it is especially important that you keep up with any developments and changes in the field. A leave of absence from the workforce isn't an excuse to ignore current events.

Knowing about a company's past is important, but you also want to know about its present. It is imperative to stay on top of the latest news about your prospective employer, the industry, and your profession. Find out if there are any changes on the horizon, such as mergers or acquisitions, and what effect these changes will have on the company and its employees. You should learn whether the company has released any new products lately and how the public has reacted to these products. You should be aware of any changes that are occurring in the industry and in your profession as well.

Finally, don't walk into your interview without details about the job for which you are a candidate. If you don't have a job announcement, check the employer's website to see if you can find one there. It is perfectly appropriate for you to ask for a detailed job description when the employer calls to invite you to come in for an interview. The more you know about the job, the better you will be able to demonstrate to the employer that you are the best person to fill it.

Where to Begin Your Research

The easiest place to begin your research is the company's website. Most entities have websites, so it should be fairly easy to find the one you're looking for. Use a search engine like Google or Yahoo! and type the organization's name in quotation marks into the search box. In addition to finding the company's official site, your results may also bring up other sites that talk about your prospective employer. Bookmark those to look at when you get further into your research. Remember that the primary purpose of a corporate website is to act as a publicity tool. The information you find there is meant to cast the company in the best possible light, so don't expect to dig up any dirt there.

 Fact

Do you want to figure out which website on your results list belongs to the company? Look at the URLs listed there—the company's URL will often include the company's name. For example, the URL for Adams Media, the publisher of this book, is *www.adams media.com.*

Next, if the organization you are researching is publicly held, meaning it has publicly traded securities, you should try to get your hands on its annual report and other corporate documents. According to United States law, most publicly held companies are required to disclose financial and other pertinent information to their shareholders and to the Securities and Exchange Commission. These companies send glossy, magazine-style annual reports to shareholders. While these reports must be accurate, companies use annual reports to present information in the best possible light. For a more detailed and more realistic look, see the reports your prospective employer files with the SEC. These corporate reports are filed after the end of a company's fiscal year, quarterly, and whenever an event warrants disclosure.

You can often find the annual report on a company's website or you can request a copy from its investor relations department. You can download most other corporate reports from the SEC's website (*www.sec.gov*). Look for an annual report called a 10-K and a quarterly report called a 10-Q.

Alert

While most publicly held companies are required to file annual, quarterly, or other reports with the SEC, some are not. Only companies that have more than $10 million in assets and securities held by more than 500 owners must file these reports. If the company for which you need information is relatively small, you will have to turn to other sources.

If a company isn't required to file an annual report, you may have a difficult time finding its financial reports. Privately held companies are under no requirement to disclose that information; therefore, they often don't. With a little digging you might be able to find limited financial information about your prospective employer, such as annual sales.

Company Directories

One place to look for information about an organization's finances is in a company directory. These are encyclopedia- or dictionary-style resources that contain entries on many different companies. While they don't contain a wealth of information, they do cover the basics. For example, you should be able to learn about a company's products and services, its monetary value, its key personnel, and its organizational structure.

Some company directories are available online. Occasionally, limited access is available at no charge, but there are fees for more extensive access. These directories are referred to as proprietary databases and are often available at public and college libraries. Some of these libraries even allow their patrons to search these databases from their home computers. For more about that, consult with your library. Your librarian can tell you which ones they have and how you can access them.

Keeping Up with the News

Annual reports, corporate documents, and company directories are great resources, but they have a down side. The information contained in them is generally outdated by the time they are published. To say nothing ever stays the same entirely understates reality. In your research, you learned that your prospective employer manufactures a particular product or provides a particular service. Recently, perhaps, that company has added a new product or service. Maybe that's even the reason they're hiring now. Your prospective employer may have just acquired a new subsidiary or may have been purchased by another company. Don't underestimate the importance of uncovering the latest news you can find, whether that news is positive or negative.

You can find newsworthy information for your field or industry in trade or professional publications. You should be reading these publications, either in print or on the Internet, regularly. This activity will help you learn about major events within your field, including ones that involve your prospective employer.

☀ Alert

If you learned something about your prospective employer that puts the company in a bad light, think carefully before you bring it up. However, if you need this information in order to decide whether or not to accept a job offer, ask your question as tactfully as you can. Start off by saying, "I hope this doesn't offend you, but I really need to know the answer to this question."

If you haven't been keeping up with your reading, you can access archives of these publications. Archives are sometimes available on the publisher's website or on research databases that index articles from various publications. Sometimes these articles appear in full text and can be downloaded and printed out. Sometimes you will see only the title of the article or a short abstract and will have to figure out where you can get the article you want. You may be able to purchase it from the database publisher or from the publication that originally ran the article. You may also be able to request the article from your local library. If they don't have it, they may be able to retrieve it from another library through an interlibrary loan.

Essential

Most public libraries subscribe to research databases on which you can access a variety of publications, including professional and trade publications, newspapers, business journals, and magazines. Library card holders can often use these databases, either at the library or at home. Check with your local library to find out what databases they subscribe to and how to access them.

Your quest for news about your prospective employer shouldn't end with professional or trade publications. You should also look at newspapers, business journals, and magazines. "Wait a minute," you may be thinking. "How much time do you think I have?" Of course, you can't spend an exorbitant amount of time searching through every publication that might have an article about your prospective employer. There are tools that will help you expedite this process.

NEWS SEARCH ENGINES

You can search for news stories using search engines like Google, Ask.com, and Yahoo! Each has a news search function that is separate from its regular web search function. You will find stories listed here minutes after they break. You don't have to continually search these engines for breaking news; you can receive alerts whenever the search engine picks up something new.

Depending on the search engine you use, you can receive news alerts either by e-mail or through a newsfeed. Setting up an e-mail news alert is effortless; all you need is an e-mail account. Click on the link to e-mail news alerts. For example, on Google, do a search for a particular company, click on the "New" option at the top of the search results page, and look for an envelope with the words "News Alert" under it. You will have to indicate what terms you want the search engine to monitor and how often you want to be alerted when those terms are found.

 **Question**

What newsfeed reader should I use?
Bloglines (*www.bloglines.com*) is a popular newsfeed reader. Once you set up an account, you can subscribe to newsfeeds and blogs. Google Reader, available on the Google website (*www .google.com*), is another newsfeed reader. You must sign up for a Google account to use it.

Setting up a newsfeed takes some more effort since you will have to sign up for a newsfeed reader or aggregator. A newsfeed reader is a piece of software that goes to the sites to which you've subscribed and collects newly added content on your topic for you to read. This is an invaluable tool if you plan to subscribe to several news alerts from different sources. It is also a must if you subscribe to any blogs, which will be discussed later. There are web-based newsfeed readers that you access via a website, as well as ones that you install on your computer.

Once you have signed up for a newsfeed reader, you can subscribe to a newsfeed. First perform your search and then, on your results page, look for a link to subscribe to the feed. It may say RSS (it stands for Really Simple Syndication), Atom, or "subscribe to this search." Clicking on the link will bring you to the subscription page of your newsfeed reader.

Alert

A blog kept by an employee or former employee may be filled with gossip, but you may be able to find some grains of truth. Read these blogs with a critical eye, remembering there may be inaccuracies in them. Disgruntled former employees, for example, may not say the nicest of things. Some statements may be true and others may not.

BLOGS

You will also use a newsfeed reader to subscribe to and read blogs. A blog is an abbreviation for web log, and it is traditionally an online journal or diary. Although in the past blogs were maintained primarily by people who wanted to share details of their personal lives or opinions on any number of topics, they have moved into the mainstream over the last few years. Now, corporations maintain official blogs and often link to them on their websites. You can find company news there, or at least news that the company wants to share with the general public. In addition to reading official company blogs, you should be very interested in perusing blogs maintained by employees—or former employees.

You can easily find blogs about any topic using blog search engines. Google and Ask.com both have blog search engines among their tools. Technorati (*www.technorati.com*) is a search engine dedicated specifically to blogs. In addition to finding complete blogs on your topic, you can also find individual posts on blogs that cover more general topics. If you locate a blog you find interesting, you can subscribe to it.

Take Time to Rehearse

To prepare for job interviews, it is important that you do some practice interviewing, both alone and with others. Rehearsing for interviews will allow you to work on any problems that an interviewer may view as negatives. Rehearsing will also allow you to become more comfortable with the interview process. By the time you go on an interview, you will have no problem confidently answering questions.

The interview is not only about what you say, but also about how you say it. It is difficult to see yourself as you appear to others. When you are engaged in conversation with someone, do you tend to look disinterested or do you generally look engaged? Do you look nervous or calm? Do you talk too fast, too slowly, too softly, or too loudly? You probably don't know the answers to these questions unless someone has pointed out a problem to you in the past.

To get a glimpse of what you look like when you are having a conversation with someone, you might want to begin rehearsing for your job interview in front of a mirror. Study your body language. Are your hands clasped tightly in your lap? Are your arms folded across your chest? Are you smiling? Remember your body language speaks volumes, so take a look at Chapter 2 to find out what is appropriate and what to avoid.

Next, recruit a friend to help you rehearse for job interviews. If you know someone who has experience interviewing others, especially someone who is responsible for hiring, ask him to work with you. If that person is unavailable, find someone else whose opinion you trust. Have him ask you questions and then answer them as if you were on an actual interview. To make the situation more realistic, have your friend choose the questions to ask.

 Fact

Toastmasters International is a nonprofit organization dedicated to helping people strengthen their communication skills. Members receive help in areas such as organization, voice inflection, and persuasiveness. There are more than 9,300 Toastmasters clubs located around the world. You can find one near you by going to *www.toastmasters.org.*

If you have several friends who are job hunting, you can all practice interviewing together. Videotape yourselves interviewing one another and then play back the tapes. Critique one another's performances as well as your own. Once you get through that, the real thing will seem so much easier.

Access Your Network

A network is a group of individuals to whom you can turn for help. Your network may consist of people you've worked with in the past, your friends, and your relatives. These people have networks of their own and may know someone else who can give you advice. Eventually, if you branch out far enough, you're bound to find someone who knows something about one of the companies you're interested in.

Most people think of their networks only when they are trying to find out about employment opportunities. However, a great time to access your network is when you have been asked to come in for a job interview. Some members of your network may have worked for the company you are interviewing with, and others may know someone who has worked there or currently works there. Someone in your network may have interviewed there in the past or may know the person who is interviewing you.

Imagine all the valuable information you can get from someone who has had some sort of contact with the company you are interviewing with. You can learn things you would not be able to learn anywhere else. Sure, you can use other resources to learn about a company's finances or to find up-to-date news. Someone on your network, though, may be able to tell you that the person who is interviewing you will be very impressed by the fact that you speak four languages and will tell you not to wear anything green because the interviewer really hates it.

Alert

Be cautious about revealing anything you learned through your network. If you start talking about something that wasn't released to the public, the interviewer will want to know how you got your information. Your network can be valuable for gaining background information about your prospective employer and for getting an inside peek at its work environment.

Dealing with Anxiety

Interviews make a lot of people nervous. Levels of anxiety vary from mild to severe, and anxiety can sabotage your performance on a job interview. Since what many people fear most is the unknown, preparing for a job interview can help alleviate this feeling. With that said, you may still have butterflies fluttering around in your stomach even after becoming as familiar as possible with the interview process, learning what questions to anticipate and how you will answer them, and rehearsing for the interview. Remember that you've done everything you can to prepare. Because of that, you have tremendously increased your chances of succeeding. You should be able to walk into the interview calm, cool, collected, and bursting with confidence. However, you won't be able to do that if you aren't relaxed. Don't let your anxiety take away from your performance on a job interview. Find a way to relieve your stress before it affects your chances of getting the job you want.

People use many techniques to relieve stress. You should know which techniques work well for you and utilize them in the days leading up to your job interview. Many people swear by exercise as a great way to relieve anxiety. If exercise is one of the ways you de-stress, an early morning run before an interview or a workout at the gym may help you. If strenuous exercise isn't something you are used to, it may not be wise to start a new exercise regimen the day of your interview. Perhaps you should take a tension-relieving walk in the park or around town instead. You can also try massage therapy, meditation, or deep-breathing exercises.

 Fact

When people are asked to rank life events in order of the level of stress, a change in employment is consistently ranked as one of the highest stressors on that list. With that in mind, it's perfectly normal to be anxious about a job interview.

What to Do about Low Confidence

Sometimes job searches can take a very long time. This is especially true during economic downturns. People are sometimes out of work for months or even a year at a time. This can be very rough on a person's ego. If you are in this situation, your confidence may wane and you may doubt whether you will ever find a job.

Your lack of confidence will be very visible to anyone you come into contact with—including prospective employers. You must get out of your slump and do it fast, or you won't be hired—not because of a bad economy, but because of the way you carry yourself.

Zoom in on your accomplishments. Remember all the great things you did in your career. Think about what you can bring to a new job. Think about how lucky any employer would be to have you work for her. Focus on these things, and the interviewer will notice them too.

⟩⟨Ε⟩⟨ Alert

Do whatever you can to boost your confidence. If you are nervous during a job interview, you won't look confident and will be too distracted to answer questions to the best of your ability. If you are anxious in the days leading up to an interview, you will lose sleep and won't be well rested.

The Night Before and Morning of the Interview

Even if you wouldn't describe it as anxiety, you may not feel completely calm the night before an interview. You are human, after all. Spend a relaxing evening at home. Soaking in a hot tub or curling up with a good book is sure to calm you down. If you can, try not to think too much about the job interview. Have some caffeine-free herbal tea to help you relax. Remember, caffeine can be found in substances other than coffee, including chocolate and many over-the-counter medications. Read labels carefully. When in doubt, avoid taking anything that may act as a stimulant and keep you from getting a good night's sleep.

Get to bed early if possible. You will want to have a full night's sleep so you appear well rested for the interview. Dark circles under the eyes never enhanced anyone's looks. If you are sleepy, you won't be alert and you may have difficulty paying attention during the interview.

Give yourself plenty of time in the morning to get ready. If you have to rush around, you will only add to your anxiety. Be ready to deal with any problems you didn't anticipate, like a run in your stockings or a stain on your favorite shirt. Make sure you have backups.

Don't forget to eat a good breakfast before you leave the house. Nutritionists have lectured for years that this is the best way to start your day off right. If you are hungry, you won't be able to concentrate. Besides, a growling stomach during a job interview would be very embarrassing.

Don't overdo your coffee consumption the day of your interview. Many people get jittery from even a little too much caffeine. Of course, the day of your interview is not the time to go off caffeine cold turkey. You should have a cup of coffee if you need it to get you going, but don't have two, three, or four cups. If you are already feeling a little nervous, this will just exacerbate it.

Finally, take a moment to concentrate on the job for which you are interviewing. Tell yourself why you like the job, and repeat your strengths to yourself. This will give you a positive start to the day, and you'll be able to go to the interview confident and focused.

Chapter 2

First Impressions Count

YOU HAVE WORKED hard researching your prospective employer and you know what you need to say to convince him you are the best candidate for the job. But there's one more thing to think about before the big day—the first impression. Your physical appearance, what you do when you meet the interviewer, and your body language during the interview all contribute to the opinion your interviewer will form of you. Be prepared to make a great first impression even before you open your mouth.

What to Wear to the Interview

Most people are troubled by the thought of what to wear for a job interview. They wonder if they should wear casual clothes or formal attire. They question whether to choose bright colors or neutral tones. Even among fashionistas, there is quite a bit of disagreement over what is appropriate to wear for a job interview.

Some experts feel that regardless of the culture of the company, a person should always wear a suit for an interview. Other experts feel that wearing a suit is not necessary in some situations; worse, it could even be inappropriate. Are you even more confused now? Don't be. Here are some pointers to help you decide on an outfit that will help you shine on a job interview.

When Should You Wear a Suit?

If you are interviewing for a job in a traditionally conservative field, such as accounting, finance, or law, the answer to the question "What should I wear?" is a simple one. Both men and women must wear suits. You should choose a conservative color such as black, gray, or navy blue.

Invest in at least two suits. If you buy two, you won't have to worry about what to wear when you get called back for a second interview. You will also be a step ahead when you get a job offer and those suits become a regular part of your wardrobe. Buy a conservative rather than a trendy suit and always buy the best quality you can afford. You can wear the same suit for several years if you stick to these rules.

Fact

If you want to get the best prices on business attire, remember that men's suits are often on sale during April and November. Men's shirts go on sale in January and July, and the best months to buy shoes are January, July, November, and December.

Underneath the suit, you should wear a solid, preferably white or light-colored, shirt or blouse. A man should wear a necktie. A woman can accessorize with a silk scarf if she wishes. Both ties and scarves should have simple designs and should not be brightly colored. Women's scarves should be of short or medium length since a long scarf could get in her way.

Is Casual Dress Ever Appropriate?

As you can see, your choices of what to wear are limited when you are interviewing in a conservative field. That is not necessarily a bad thing—at least it makes your decision easy. Just ask anyone who is interviewing for a job in a field where the mode of dress is not so clearly defined. The definition of proper interview attire in a casual office is something not all experts agree on, whether you ask those who work in fashion or those who work in career planning.

While some people feel that a formal suit is appropriate for all job interviews, others feel that what you wear on an interview should be similar to what you will wear on the job should you be hired. When you have a job interview, you want the interviewer to envision you as a member of his staff. The way you dress can help him do that.

Of course, a job interview should be considered a special occasion and not just a typical day at the office. Therefore, your attire should be a notch or two above what you would wear to work. If, for example, typical dress in the workplace you're interested in joining is casual, you should opt for dress pants and a coordinating sport jacket for men, and dress pants, a skirt, or a dress and coordinated blazer for women.

A company's corporate culture usually dictates how employees dress. You can try to learn more about a prospective employer's corporate culture from the research you do in preparation for the job interview. Companies in more creative industries usually have less stringent dress codes.

Essential

If you can't find a company's dress code standards through traditional research, hanging out near the building's entrance at the beginning of a work day will allow you to see what people look like when they arrive for work. Avoid doing this on a Friday, as that is the day of the week many companies allow casual dress.

If you have exhausted all ways of finding out how employees of the company dress, you might have to wear a suit. If given the choice between overdressing for a job interview and underdressing for one, you are better off being overdressed. In other words, it is more acceptable to be the only job candidate who shows up in a suit rather than the only one who does not.

The Finer Details

More important than what you wear to a job interview is how you wear it. Check your clothing to make sure it is stain-free. Also make sure it is unwrinkled. The last thing you want is to look like you rolled out of the hamper. It is worth bringing your suit to the dry cleaner to have it professionally cleaned and pressed.

Alert

Women should make sure their hosiery is free of runs and visible snags. Carry an extra pair in your purse just in case. Men should make sure their tie is straight. Invest in a tie tack to keep it in place.

Women should stay away from low-cut necklines or skirts with short hemlines. Revealing outfits may be fine for an evening out after work, but they are not appropriate for the office—any office. Suits should fit properly. That means they should not be too tight or too baggy. If your outfit does not fit you well, a trip to the tailor is in order.

Hair, Makeup, and Nails

Your hair should be neat and clean. The style should be simple. Women's makeup should not be overdone. Lipstick and nail polish should be a neutral color. Women's nails should be short enough to keep the interviewer from wondering, "How will she get work done with those nails?" Men's nails should be short and clean. Men should be clean-shaven. If you have facial hair, it should be neatly trimmed.

Guidelines for Jewelry

Both men and women should keep jewelry to a bare minimum. That means large dangling earrings, big pendants, and thick chains are out. While body piercings and tattoos may be all the rage in your social circle, remember that some interviewers will be turned off by this. While you are allowed to have your own personal style, a job interview may not be the best place for you to express it. You certainly do not want anything to distract the interviewer from realizing you are the best candidate for the job.

Your Shoes

Finally, it's time to think about your feet, or rather what you are going to put on them. Your shoes are the last thing you will put on before you head off on an interview, but they should not be the last thing you should think about. On the contrary, you should give serious consideration to your footwear.

Shoes that are conservative in both style and color are the most appropriate to wear on a job interview. Neither men nor women should wear sandals or open-toed shoes of any kind. Black shoes go with everything, even with navy blue, according to fashion experts.

 Fact

> One of the first things some job interviewers notice is the condition of a candidate's shoes. Scuffed, dirty shoes may indicate that the person doesn't pay attention to detail. You can purchase shoe polish and other shoe care supplies at your local drug store.

Shoes must be in good condition. They do not have to be brand-new, but they should not look like you have hiked miles in them, either. They shouldn't have scuffs on them. If they do, go ahead and polish them. If you do buy new shoes for interviewing, make sure they are comfortable. It is hard to concentrate on the task at hand when your toes are being pinched. Excessively high heels are out of place on a job interview and in the workplace.

What to Bring to the Interview

Once you are dressed appropriately, you are ready to walk into the interview with confidence. There are a few things you should always have with you. First and foremost, always bring along a few copies of your resume. The interviewer may want a fresh copy and you may be introduced to other people who will need a copy as well. In order to keep your resumes clean and neat, put them in a folder to transport them to the interview.

You may have a portfolio of work samples. If the interviewer has asked to see them or if you think they are noteworthy, bring them with you. Make sure they are neatly compiled and organized. They should represent your best work.

Essential

Arrange your work samples in a binder. The binder should be a conservative color, such as black or navy, and it should be in good condition. Insert your documents into plastic sheet protectors, which you can find at all office supply stores.

Always carry a pen and a small notebook in case there is something you want to jot down. Do not forget to bring your date book so you can schedule any future appointments.

Carry your resumes, portfolio, and other items in a briefcase. Women may also carry small purses. In general, though, you should travel light. Women should not carry large, bulky handbags or anything that looks better suited for a day at the beach. No one should carry a backpack, and shopping bags are definitely out.

Getting to the Interview on Time

There is one thing you can do to sabotage your chances of getting hired even before you shake the interviewer's hand. If you arrive late for the interview, you might as well write your own rejection letter. Your prospective employer will be offended. Even showing up exactly on time is a bad idea. Running in at the last minute will throw you off, and you will not perform as well as you might have had you arrived with a few minutes to spare. There are a few things you can do to reduce your risk of being late.

 Fact

If you have access to the Internet, you can plan your trip online. Use mapping websites to plan your trip if you're driving. Many municipal transit systems have their schedules and routes online. You can type in your starting point and your destination, using landmarks, addresses, or intersections to plan your trip.

When a prospective employer calls to ask you to come in for an interview, be sure to find out exactly where the interview will take place. Some companies have offices in more than one location. These addresses can be across town or merely across the street from one another. Regardless of the distance between them, you do not want to waste time wandering from one place to another.

Once you know where you have to go, you have to figure out how to get there. If you are driving, map out a route and, if possible, an alternate route just in case you hit some traffic snags along the way. If you have to take a train or a bus, make sure you know which lines you have to ride and which ones you can ride instead if something should happen to interrupt service.

You should plan to arrive for your interview early. It is best to get there at least 10 or 15 minutes before your scheduled appointment.

If you decide to be an early bird, though, do not show up inside your prospective employer's office any more than 10 to 15 minutes prior to your appointment. Doing so may make the interviewer feel like you are pressuring her to start the interview early.

Arriving for Your Appointment

Announce yourself to the receptionist as soon as you arrive at your prospective employer's offices. Many people do not realize how important this part is. The receptionist is the first employee of the company with whom you will have contact. As a matter of fact, he is the first person every person arriving for an interview meets.

Do not discount the power this person wields. The interviewer may rely on the receptionist to give an opinion of the job candidates. That is one reason it is imperative that you be on your very best behavior right from the start. You might also wind up working with this person.

Politely walk up to the reception desk and give the receptionist your name and the name of the person with whom you have an appointment. You can make small talk about the weather or traffic if you wish. Remember, if you are kept waiting, do not complain to the receptionist or become argumentative with him.

While you are waiting to be called in for the interview, spend your time wisely. You can look over your resume and review any notes you may have prepared. If you finish doing that and still have not been called in, take a look at the professional journals that may be available in the waiting area. Do not bring out the novel you brought along to read on the train. You want to look like you are busy, not as if you are relaxing.

The Interview Begins

Usually the receptionist will announce your arrival to the interviewer and she will come out to the waiting area to greet you. This is the only chance you will have to make a good first impression. While your behavior during the interview is important, a bad first impression will be very difficult to overcome.

Meeting the Interviewer

When you first meet the interviewer, you must appear confident, but not smug. You should be assertive, but not aggressive. You should be friendly, but not overly familiar.

When the interviewer comes out to greet you, the first thing you should do is introduce yourself to him using your first and last name. Do not address him by his first name. Your introduction should sound something like this (feel free to use your own variation): "Hello, Mr. Smith. I'm Joan Brown. It's nice to meet you." You should be ready to shake his hand, but do not offer your hand first. Doing so can put you in an awkward situation if the interviewer does not offer his hand in return.

 Fact

As you proceed to the site of the interview, the interviewer may try to make small talk. Stick to things like the weather and stay away from how your favorite team played last night. Your favorite team may turn out to be his team's archrival, which could result in an awkward moment you don't really need at this point.

Getting Started

Once you arrive in the office where your interview will be held, etiquette dictates that you wait for the interviewer to offer you a seat. However, just because someone is in a position to interview you does not mean he has manners. If the interviewer sits down without first offering you a seat, sit down across from him or wherever there is an available seat. He is probably in a hurry to get the interview started, so do not waste any time. Get the copies of your resume, portfolio, notebook, and pen ready so you will not have to fumble around trying to find them later.

Body Language

When you interact with other people, there are two ways your message comes through to them. You consciously convey your message through your words. Your body language unconsciously sends signals as well. Body language is comprised of the nonverbal gestures and mannerisms that may indicate a person's true feelings.

Your body language can reveal things that your words do not. In fact, it may reveal much more than you intend to reveal. In the simplest terms, if you say you are happy but have a big frown on your face, your body language—the frown—will show your true feelings. While most people manage to exert a great deal of control over the words they let cross their lips, many have difficulty when it comes to keeping their body language in check.

Essential

Participate in videotaped mock job interviews and analyze your body language afterward. Once you are able to see how you interact with others, you can work on identifying and eliminating any undesirable behaviors that may be distracting in a job interview.

You may think all this talk about body language is just a bunch of nonsense. However, you must pay attention to what your body language seems to reveal even if you question whether there is any truth to it. Many interviewers are trained to look for even the subtlest nonverbal cues and interpret what they mean. Whether these interpretations are correct is irrelevant; what the interviewer believes is what counts. Read the following section carefully. If you have a habit of doing any of the following behaviors or something else that may make you appear anxious or disinterested, you need to extinguish it.

Stay Calm—or at Least Look That Way

A job interview is very stressful for many people. Your anxiety may be brought on by the fact that a job interview is a very unnatural situation. How often do you sit across from another person while he fires a series of questions at you?

It is disconcerting to be put under a microscope by another person, especially when your livelihood may depend on the outcome of that person's research. Since one of your goals on a job interview is to appear confident, the last thing you want to do is let your body language betray your anxiety.

 Fact

Most people have some sort of behavior that appears when they are feeling anxious. One person may twirl the end of her hair or chew her bottom lip, another may wring his hands, and someone else may twist a ring around her finger or play with a pendant. Try to identify your own individual anxious behavior and keep it in check during the interview.

What to Do with Your Hands and Arms

Many people do not know what to do with their hands and arms during an interview. Should you clasp them together or keep them at your sides? Should you hold a pen to keep your hands occupied? Should you keep your arms folded across your chest?

The best thing to do with your hands is to let them rest in your lap. You may have them clasped together, as long as you don't clasp them too tightly and appear to be trying to hold them still. Folding your arms across your chest is often seen as an indication that you are closing yourself off or putting up a barrier. Since you want to appear open and approachable on a job interview, you should avoid doing that.

Holding a pen is not necessarily bad, but be careful not to fiddle with it. Remember not to point or clench your hands into fists. Also avoid covering your mouth with your hand or touching your face when you speak.

Essential

If you tend to be shy or know that making eye contact tends to be a problem for you, you can practice making eye contact when you talk to people you are very comfortable with; for example, friends and family. Graduate to making eye contact with the cashier in the supermarket or the bank teller. Soon you should be able to accomplish this in all situations.

Make Eye Contact

If you have ever taken a public-speaking class, you no doubt discussed how important it is to make eye contact. If you avoid making eye contact, the interviewer may jump to the conclusion that you are not being truthful about something. That, of course, is the last thing you would want an interviewer to determine from your body language. He may also be wary of hiring someone who appears to have difficulty carrying on a conversation, which is another impression you must avoid making.

Sit Up Straight

How you sit during an interview is very important. Think back to when you were a child and your parents and teachers told you to sit up straight. They were not kidding. Good posture helps you look confident. Slouching makes you look lazy and bored.

Sitting up straight also makes it easier to breathe, as any yoga instructor will tell you. Many people tend to forget to breathe when they are in a stressful situation, and they let out a huge sigh when they remember. This is not a good idea during an interview.

It is preferable to keep your feet flat on the floor, but you can also have them crossed at the ankles. Do not cross your legs at the knee or have your ankle resting on your opposite knee. You should lean forward slightly. This shows that you are an eager participant in the conversation.

The Handshake

Another important thing to think about is the handshake. The opportunity for a handshake presents itself at two points in a job interview. The first time is when you meet the interviewer. The other is at the end of the interview when you are getting ready to leave.

Fact

Some men get all wishy-washy when it comes time to shake hands with a woman. While it is true that a woman's hands may be more delicate than a man's, it is unlikely that your handshake will cause any damage. If you think it might, then you need to loosen up, whether you are shaking a man's or a woman's hand.

The moment when a handshake can take place can be somewhat awkward; for instance, if you put out your hand and the gesture is not reciprocated. However, if the interviewer puts out her hand and you are not ready to shake her hand at that moment, you will be putting her in an awkward situation. That is certainly something you want to avoid.

Therefore, while you do not want to initiate the handshake, make sure you are ready for it by keeping your right hand free at your side, ready to move into the handshake position. Don't hold anything in your right hand as you enter and leave the office. When you do shake hands, your handshake should be firm, which demonstrates that you are confident.

Making Your Exit

Just as your arrival at the interview provides you with your first opportunity to make a good impression, your exit provides you with the chance to make a lasting one. What you do at this point may be what sticks in the interviewer's mind when it is time to decide who to hire. Make sure you end the interview on a positive note.

Do You Have Any Questions?

At the end of the interview, the interviewer will usually ask you if you have any questions. "No" is not a good answer. This is your chance to become a proactive part of the job interview, so don't waste it. The purpose of the questions you ask is twofold. They should indicate your interest in the job. They should also help you learn as much as you can to help you make an informed decision if you are offered the job. You should come to the interview with a list of prepared questions to ask the interviewer.

Alert

When asking your prospective employer questions at the end of your interview, you should not ask questions about salary, vacations, or benefits. All of these topics are best left for when the employer offers you the job. It is more polite, and you will be in a better position to negotiate once you have received an offer.

You can ask the interviewer to clarify the job duties or explain the chain of command. You can also ask him for more information about something he mentioned during the interview. You will find a list of suggested questions you can ask in Chapter 14.

Ask for the Job

Don't forget to ask for the job before you leave. Most people neglect to do this. They may not want to appear overly eager. However, the interviewer is not a mind reader. If you do not let him know you want the job, he may assume you have decided you don't want it.

You do not have to come out and say, "I want the job." You can say instead, "Based on what we discussed today, I think I would be a perfect fit for this job. When can I expect to hear from you?" This statement not only expresses your interest in the job, but also gives you the opportunity to reiterate that you are qualified to fill the position.

Before you leave, do not forget to say goodbye to the interviewer. Tell him it was nice to meet with him. As you did when you first began, be ready to shake the interviewer's hand if he extends it.

Interviewing over a Meal

When you find out your interview is going to take place over a meal, you may get indigestion before you even begin to eat. It is not enough to have to worry about impressing a potential employer with your words and avoiding any revealing body language. Now you also have to worry about using the right fork, not spilling soup on yourself, and not having food stuck between your teeth. Here are some tips that will help you survive such an interview.

Sitting Down at the Table

When you arrive at the table, wait for everyone to sit down before you do, unless of course someone signals you to sit down first. After you sit down at the table, you should place your napkin on your lap. Generally you want to wait for your host to do this first. If the napkin is a large dinner-style one, you should fold it in half. If it is a small luncheon-style napkin, you can unfold it completely.

There may be a basket of bread on the table. If it is in front of you, offer it to your dining companions before you help yourself. If it is not in front of you, wait until others have helped themselves before you ask someone to pass it to you. Do not reach in front of anyone or across the table to get it.

Place bread on your bread plate, which should be the smallest plate at your setting. Use your butter knife, or your regular knife if you do not have a butter knife, to place a piece of butter on your bread plate. Then break off a bite-sized piece of bread, apply the butter to it, and eat that piece. Do not butter an entire slice of bread or roll at once and proceed to eat it like a sandwich.

Ⓔ Fact

Place settings will often include a variety of utensils. Many people are confused about what to use first, second, and so forth. The rule of thumb is to start furthest away from your plate and work your way in as the meal progresses.

What to Order

When the waitress arrives to take drink orders, make yours a soda or water. While an alcoholic beverage may calm you down, it may also loosen you up—too much. If your host orders a bottle of wine for the table, refusing to have some may appear rude. In that case, allow the waiter to pour some for you, but sip it slowly.

When it comes time to order your meal, choose wisely. Stay away from any messy foods. Spaghetti is out. Avoid foods that tend to get stuck in your teeth, like spinach or poppy seeds. Choose something that is moderately priced. Your prospective employer is footing the bill and you do not want to look greedy.

The Meal

When the food begins to arrive, wait until everyone is served before you begin eating. When you cut up your food, use both your knife and fork to cut off one piece at a time. Do not hold your knife in your hand while you are eating and do not put a used utensil down on the table. Place your knife on your plate until you are ready to use it again.

Use your napkin to remove any crumbs from your face. Remember to dab and not wipe. When you are done eating, place your napkin on the table. It should be folded neatly, not crumpled up. Then politely wait for everyone else to finish.

Essential

Carry a travel-sized toothbrush and toothpaste with you to use after the meal. You should be able to find a compact model that will fit in your purse or pocket so you can go to the restroom to remove any food you fear is lodged between your teeth.

Don't Talk with Your Mouth Full

With your table manners in order, you can begin dealing with questions. The biggest question on your mind may be "How do I eat and answer questions at the same time?" With the finesse of a dentist, your interviewer may have a knack for asking you questions just as you put each forkful of food into your mouth. No matter how much you want to answer his question, remember what your mom told you—don't talk with your mouth full. It only takes a few seconds to chew and swallow, although it may seem like an eternity to you. Also remember to completely answer each question before you continue to eat.

Finishing Up

When your host places her napkin on the table, it is a signal that the meal is over. You do not want to keep her there any longer than necessary. This may or may not mean the end of the interview. Follow the interviewer's lead. When the interview is over, do what you would do at the end of a regular interview, with the addition of thanking her for the meal.

Interviewing in a Foreign Country

In today's global marketplace it is possible that you could wind up interviewing for a job in a foreign country. If this happens, you will have to learn about the culture of that country since a breach of etiquette could be interpreted as rudeness. You will have to learn about things like the proper way to greet someone, whether it is appropriate to look someone in the eye, and good table manners. The following guidelines will get you started.

 **Question**

Where can I find out more about the rules of etiquette for a specific country?

Many books have been written about cross-cultural rules of etiquette. Check your local library or the Internet for specific information on the country you are visiting. Appendix A includes a list of resources.

Be sure you know the proper method of greeting for the country you are visiting. In some cultures, people bow when they meet one another. To complicate matters further, different bows mean different things. You should make a point of learning the meaning of each one in order to avoid making any missteps.

Certain body language, while acceptable in one culture, may be considered rude in another. For example, it is considered rude to look someone directly in the eye in some countries. What is appropriate for men in a particular culture may be inappropriate for women.

If you are interviewing in another country, it is very likely that you will be faced with an interview over a meal. You may be served unfamiliar foods, some of which you may not like or may not be familiar with. When torn between being polite and being nauseated, it is okay not to eat something you find repulsive. However, you should accept what is offered; just don't put it in your mouth. You should also become familiar with the table manners that are appropriate in that culture.

Chapter 3

Revealing Your Personality

YOU'VE MET THE interviewer, shaken his hand, and now you're settling into your seat. Okay, bring it on. You're ready for anything he's going to ask. You can talk about each job you've had, your skills, and your accomplishments. Suddenly you find yourself fielding a barrage of personal questions. The interviewer is asking about things that seem to have nothing to do with work. Why does he need to know so much about you?

Why the Personal Questions?

Why would an employer want to know what you like doing for fun, your strengths and weaknesses, and even how many siblings you grew up with? Then along comes the most dreaded request: "So, tell me about yourself." Your heart begins to pound so loudly you're sure the interviewer can hear it. "Tell you about myself? Have you got a few hours?"

Be assured the interviewer usually doesn't want to know all the private details of your life. As a matter of fact, he doesn't have the right to ask for that kind of information. What a prospective employer is interested in learning about are your personal qualities, or your character traits. This information will help him decide whether to hire you.

Basically, the prospective employer wants to know if you have what it takes to work at his company. Yes, you may have the skills and experience, but do you have the personality? Aspects of your personality are a strong indicator of whether you will be a good employee. The interviewer wants to know whether or not you procrastinate, are discreet, and are a team player. He wants to know if you work well on your own and how you make decisions, handle stress, and solve problems.

Before beginning the interviewing process, a hiring manager may have gone through hundreds of resumes looking for candidates who have the skills and experience required for the job in question. The interviewer's job now is to be a detective. He wants to know what makes you a better choice than another candidate who has the same experience and skills.

⚡ Alert

Don't reveal more about yourself than is necessary during a job interview. While you should be honest with the interviewer, don't tell her more than she needs to know. Revealing too much information can get you into trouble.

An interviewer will try to learn about your personality by asking you either direct questions, e.g., "Do you tend to begin a project as soon as it is assigned or do you begin working as you get close to the deadline?" or by asking you questions that get you to reveal this information, e.g., "Tell me how you approach a new project." Give careful consideration to every question the interviewer asks. He has a reason for asking every one of them. Figuring out the reason for each question can help you give the best answer.

Now, let's get back to the dreaded question: "Tell me about yourself." The interviewer doesn't want your memoirs. The rule of thumb is to keep it simple. The interviewer is interested only in knowing whether you have the skills and qualities necessary to fulfill the requirements of the position for which you are interviewing. Interviewees sometimes make the mistake of revealing too much when what the prospective employer really wants to know is "Can you do the job?" and "Will you fit in here?"

Questions and Answers

Q Tell me about yourself.

A I attended Ace Business College, where I earned my associate's degree in office technology five years ago. I started working as a library clerk right after I graduated, and I was promoted to assistant circulation manager after a year. I helped the library switch over to a new circulation system about two years ago. I was part of the team that selected the new system and I helped train our department in its use. In addition to my technical skills, I am adept at troubleshooting. I also work well with customers, helping to solve any problems that arise. I'm now ready to take on a job with more responsibility and I know I will make a great circulation manager.

This candidate tells the interviewer about his skills and experience and shows why he is qualified for the job. He doesn't wander off course or reveal information that is irrelevant. Although this answer is a bit long, it is to the point and tells the interviewer only what she needs to know.

Never Say: "I was born in Wisconsin, one of three children. I did well in school. I was on the football team and editor of my high school newspaper. I moved to Chicago to go to college and . . ." The interviewer doesn't want your life story. Keep your answer limited to the parts that will affect your suitability for the job.

Q Do you work well on your own?

A Yes, I do. I'm very focused and efficient.

This is a very simple and honest answer. Most jobs will require you to work on your own sometimes, if not all the time.

Never Say: "I would much rather work on my own." In addition to sometimes working on your own, many jobs also require you to be part of a team at times. Don't volunteer information that makes you seem difficult to work with; just answer the question.

Q What do you consider to be your biggest weakness?

A I am very dedicated to my job and I expect the same level of dedication from other people. Not everyone feels the same way about work and sometimes my expectations are too high.

Wouldn't every boss love such a dedicated employee? This interviewee knew he had to find a weakness that his prospective employer would see as a strength. Another option is to pick a weakness that is somewhat innocuous, such as your love of chocolate.

Never Say: "I don't have any weaknesses." Oh, come on. Who's going to believe that?

Q What would your friends say is your biggest weakness?

A Whenever my friends and I travel together, I do a lot of advanced planning. Most of my travel companions appreciate it, but some find it annoying. We just went to the Southwest, and three months before we were going I had already put together a list of all the things we had to see. I kept everyone going all day long, every single day. In the end we all had a great time.

This candidate chooses to talk about something that could be perceived as a weakness but that also demonstrates her skills. By giving this answer she demonstrates three skills—planning, research, and strong leadership qualities. Some of her friends may not appreciate her advanced planning, which is why she considers this a weakness, but she also shows that everything worked out in the end.

Never Say: "I never see my friends because I'm always working." You know what they say about all work and no play. A little time away from the office is good for everyone.

Q How do you handle success?

A I give myself a quick pat on the back and move on to the next project. Of course, I take the time to figure out what helped me succeed and use that experience to help me the next time.

This prospective employee takes appropriate pride in his success but also believes in the old adage "Don't rest on your laurels." He also learns from his experience.

Never Say: "I make sure everyone knows about it. If I don't brag about my own success, then who will?" That's true, but there are more subtle ways of getting the word out. Besides, if he's so busy bragging, who's doing all his work?

Q How do you handle failure?

A I give myself a short time to feel sad, but I don't dwell on it. Who has time for that? I don't spend too much energy on my failures, but I always try to figure out where things went wrong. If I don't do that, I won't know what I need to do to succeed next time.

This isn't someone who wastes any time feeling sorry for herself. She's also smart enough to learn from her mistakes.

Never Say: "I never fail, so I don't have to handle it." Everyone has failures, so the interviewer can only assume this candidate is lying or joking. Either way, she may be able to count this interview among her failures.

Q What are your long-term goals?

A I want to move into a supervisory position eventually. I know that will take time and hard work, but it is something I expect to achieve.

That's a good answer as long as the applicant isn't implying that he wants the interviewer's job. Making the interviewer feel threatened will not win him any points. It's important to emphasize not only that you have goals, but that you are willing to do the work to reach them.

Never Say: "I want to run this place." Wait. Doesn't the interviewer run this place?

Q What are your short-term goals?

A I want to work for a growing company in a position that allows me to use my skills to help that growth. I know your company is trying to expand into the teen market. My experience selling to that market will help your company reach its goals.

This interviewee's goals are aligned with those of the company. By giving an example of how she will help the company meet its goals, she has forced the employer to visualize her as an employee. This answer also shows that the interviewee took the time to research the company before her appointment.

Never Say: "I plan to begin working on my MBA as soon as possible." While this interviewee is clearly ambitious, she hasn't shown how her goals have anything to do with the job for which she's interviewing.

Q Do you prefer to work alone or as part of a team?

A Each situation is different. When I'm working on some projects, I prefer to be part of a team, while I'd rather work alone on other projects. I enjoy being part of a team, but I can work independently, too.

This interviewer shows that he's flexible and can adapt to working in either situation.

Never Say: "Teams are clearly a better use of resources. I'm a team player all the way." It's important to show flexibility because most jobs require you to be able to work independently at least some of the time, as well as on a team.

Q What do you consider to be your greatest strength?

A My greatest strength is my ability to see a project through from its inception to its completion. Each project I am assigned is important to me and I always make sure it gets the appropriate amount of attention.

Notice the interviewee said each project gets the "appropriate amount of attention" and not "all my attention." She clearly knows some projects need more attention than others and indicates that she knows how to prioritize.

Never Say: "I'm a hard worker and I always get to work on time." Getting to work on time is expected of all workers, as is being a hard worker. These are requirements of most jobs, not strengths.

Q How many siblings did you grow up with and how did that influence who you are today?

A *Answer 1:* I grew up as one of five children. When you grow up in such a large family, you must function as a team. Everyone takes on different responsibilities. Because my parents were so busy all the time, I also learned to be very independent.

A *Answer 2:* I grew up as an only child. I was very independent. When I got to school I had to learn how to share my toys with other

kids. It was a difficult lesson, but it helped me become
player.

*The interviewee, regardless of the size family in wh ... ne grew
up, shows that he can work alone or as part of a team.*

Never Say: *Answer 1:* "I grew up with five brothers and sisters. It
was always really noisy. I think that's why I love being alone now."

Never Say: *Answer 2:* "I was an only child. I got so used to being
alone that I really like it better that way." Uh-oh. Neither answer shows
that the interviewee is flexible enough to be a team player when he
needs to be.

Q Do you like to take risks or are you cautious?

A I'll take risks but I always proceed with caution, so I guess I fall
somewhere in between. I like to see what my odds are before I take a
risk. I also want to know what I stand to gain or what I stand to lose.

*This candidate is a careful decision-maker who isn't afraid to take
risks if there is a high probability of success. She also wants to make
sure the risk is worth taking. She's not a gambler, but she's not afraid
to take chances when it's appropriate to do so.*

Never Say: "I'm a risk-taker" or "I'm cautious." Most employers
want someone with a combination of these traits.

Q Do others think of you as a leader?

A I believe those who have seen me in action are confident in my
ability to lead them. Whenever we had to work in committees in my
marketing class, my fellow committee members always chose me to
be chairperson.

*This answer is honest and to the point. Although he is interview-
ing for his first job, he is able to draw on his college experience to
come up with an example.*

Never Say: "I lead and others follow." Confidence is good, but cockiness is not.

Q Do you consider yourself a leader?

A I am willing to take on responsibility, I am persuasive, and I can delegate. All these qualities make me a good leader. If a situation calls for someone to take charge, I will certainly step forward.

This interviewee states the qualities that make her a good leader but knows to tread lightly here. She wants to show she can evaluate the needs of each situation and step forward if necessary, while making it clear she's a team player.

Never Say: "Yes. I like being in charge." This candidate doesn't tell the interviewer why she is qualified to lead, but sounds determined to take a leadership position no matter who she steps on.

$\geq \overset{\backslash | /}{\underset{\diagup | \diagdown}{E}}$ Alert

Make sure to fully answer the interviewer's question. Explain yourself clearly and don't give answers that are too short, but also avoid ones that are too lengthy. Try to figure out why the interviewer has asked a particular question and prepare your answer with that in mind.

Q How do you handle pressure?

A I take a deep breath and figure out what needs to be done. Then I take care of it. One afternoon at 4 P.M., my boss came to me with a big research project that needed to be completed by the following morning. I rounded up my team and divided the project among us. We got it done with enough time to get home to sleep for a few hours before returning to work in the morning.

This interviewee has a strategy in place for dealing with pressure. He demonstrates how he dealt with one difficult situation using some valuable skills, including the abilities to delegate and work as part of a team.

Never Say: "I work best under pressure." That may be true, but this interviewee needs to elaborate.

Q Are you a procrastinator or do you like to get things done right away?

A Though I've been known to procrastinate on occasion, I don't make a habit of it. When someone hands me a project that needs to be done in a timely fashion, I will get it done.

Who hasn't procrastinated on occasion? What matters is that this candidate knows the difference between a project that can wait and one that needs to be done right away, and can finish the pressing ones in time to meet deadlines.

Never Say: "I never procrastinate." Really? This doesn't sound like an honest answer since everyone procrastinates at least some of the time. Everyone has flaws. Your goal on a job interview is to make yours not look so bad.

Q What pet peeves do you have about coworkers?

A Too much negativity has always bothered me. I think if you're going to complain you should be able to offer some solutions to fix the things you think are wrong.

By giving this answer, this candidate is saying, "I'm not a negative person. If I see a problem, I figure out how to fix it."

Never Say: "I say live and let live. They can do what they want; it doesn't bother me." It's virtually impossible to spend forty hours a week with a group of people and get along perfectly with them all the time. This candidate seems to be too easygoing. She'd rather let things slide than deal with them.

Q We're not a company that does things the same way year after year. How do you react to change?

A When it's appropriate, change is important. For example, when I heard about a new payroll system at a conference last year, I did a little investigating, found out it was better than what we were using, and recommended my employer move over to it.

This interviewee has shown that he doesn't shy away from change and even provides a good example of how he initiated it at his current job. He has also shown that he doesn't jump into change just for the sake of doing something different; instead, he does his homework first.

Never Say: "Change is great. Without it I get bored." The interviewer might wonder if the candidate's love of change includes finding a new job every other year.

Q What is the best money you ever spent?

A I really wanted to go to a school out of state, but my parents couldn't afford to send me to one, so I took a year off after high school and worked two jobs to earn enough money to cover the difference between the local school they could afford and the one I wanted to go to. It was a great experience. I got a great education and living away from home taught me to be independent.

This woman knows how to reach her goals and she's not afraid of working hard.

Never Say: "I got this awesome new sports car. It's so sharp and guys love it." Not only does this answer sound immature, it may make the interviewer question the applicant's priorities. Does she really want to hire someone who will be chasing after all the men in the office, possibly opening up the company to sexual harassment suits?

Q What was your worst purchase?

A I'm almost embarrassed to admit this. There were these boots that were popular a few years ago. They literally cost everything I earned working during the summer. I bought them, they lasted one season, and then they were out of style.

So you spent all your earnings on a pair of boots? That's pretty innocuous as far as frivolous purchases go. The interviewee makes sure to point out that it happened a few years ago when he didn't know any better, and that he has learned from the mistake.

Never Say: "I bought my girlfriend this really expensive engagement ring and then we broke up because she was seeing my best friend behind my back." This answer reveals way too much personal information.

Q What is the last thing you read?

A I just finished the latest book on management techniques by Jane Brown. I'm always trying to keep up with the latest literature in the field.

Reading is a great way to keep up with changes in one's field and this interviewee knows it. She proves that her interest in the field goes beyond the nine-to-five job.

Never Say: "My job keeps me so busy I really don't have time to read." Even if you don't have time to read for pleasure, you should have time to keep up with your professional literature if you want to be seen as a dedicated applicant.

Q Do you have any hobbies?

A I love woodworking. I've made tables, chairs, and a bookshelf. I love the satisfaction I get from taking a few pieces of wood and turning them into something I can use.

The applicant takes this opportunity to emphasize one of his strengths. This answer shows that he can see a project through from beginning to end.

Never Say: "Who has time for hobbies?" A successful job candidate must show that he is well rounded.

 **Question**

> **Should I discuss my personal likes and dislikes on a job interview?**
> Only if you can relate them to your career or to the job for which you are interviewing. For example, if a prospective employer asks what you like to read, stick to talking about professional literature.

Q How do you make decisions?

A I evaluate the situation before I decide what I need to do. If there is someone who has had experience with similar situations, I'm not afraid to ask for advice.

This interviewee isn't going to make a decision without considering it carefully. She is also very resourceful; seeking advice from people with more experience is always a good idea.

Never Say: "I usually go with my first instinct." This interviewee clearly doesn't put a lot of thought into things, including how to best answer this question.

Q What do you as an employee owe your boss and what does your boss owe you?

A I owe my boss hard work, respect, and honesty. My boss owes me respect, honesty, and recognition for my hard work.

In a world where honesty isn't always easy to find, this prospective employee is promising a rare commodity. The same can be said for respect. Hard work is a must, of course, but some employees only do the minimum. He is also clear about what he expects from his prospective employer.

Never Say: "I owe my employer everything. I'm at my boss's disposal. What do I expect in return? My salary." This may be every employer's dream employee . . . if it were true, which the interviewer knows it probably isn't.

 Fact

Interviewers are generally quite perceptive, and therefore they will know when a job candidate is giving answers that are too good to be true. It is important to frame your answers so they are as positive as possible, but don't go over the top. Keep your answers realistic.

Q I see that you worked full-time while attending graduate school. How did you manage to balance everything?

A It was difficult, but I managed not to fall behind at work or school. I worked five full days a week and took classes two evenings a week. I studied on the other three nights and on the weekends.

This candidate shows that she was determined to complete her degree, but not at the expense of her job.

Never Say: "I walked around exhausted all the time." This doesn't answer the interviewer's question or tell him anything about the candidate other than that she doesn't handle stress well.

Alert

Always pay attention and listen carefully during the interview. If you don't understand a question completely, it's okay to ask for clarification. It's better than answering incorrectly. You won't be able to answer a question properly unless you understand what the interviewer is asking you.

Q How do you feel about lying?

A I think lying has the potential to get you into trouble. It's much better to be honest and up front. If you are caught in a lie, the person you lied to will not have a reason to trust you in the future.

This interviewee doesn't just say lying is bad, but he also backs up his opinion by giving a negative result of lying.

Never Say: "I never lie." That wasn't the question.

Q Did you enjoy school as a child?

A Not really. I always got good grades but I think I was bored. Most teachers just talked at us. My favorite classes were the ones where group discussions happened frequently.

Someone who didn't like school won't necessarily be a bad employee. This interviewee is honest, and he gives a reason for the way he feels.

Never Say: "I hated school. I couldn't wait to get out of there. All those teachers telling me what to do drove me crazy." Even though this interviewee had the same experience as the previous one, he is a little too vehement about his feelings without giving an explanation.

Q Can you describe your ideal work environment?

A I want to work in an environment where I can use my presentation skills to help the company increase its client roster. It's important that I work in a fast-paced environment because I like being busy. I want to work somewhere where employees are recognized for their contributions.

Based on some research, this candidate is able to describe both the job that she's interviewing for and her potential employer. By showing that her ideal fits with what the job requires, she shows that she is the perfect fit for the position.

Never Say: "I want to work in a clean office with good lighting. I prefer to be on a lower floor. I really don't like cubicles." Even if this candidate had done her homework, and this was an accurate description of her potential employer's offices, this answer doesn't say anything about the job or her qualifications for it.

Q If you won a million dollars, what would you do?

A I know some people would say they'd quit their jobs and go off to some island, but they haven't considered the fact that a million dollars won't take you very far. Besides, I find this type of work fulfilling. I'd probably take a nice vacation and buy a new car. Then I'd go back to work and invest the rest of the money.

This interviewee is practical, a trait a prospective employer should find valuable.

Never Say: "I would quit my job and move to the south of France." Aside from the fact that this applicant is saying he'd leave his job if something better came along, he isn't very practical.

Q Why did you choose this career?

A When I started college, I wasn't sure what I wanted to do. I visited the career office and they gave me some self-assessment tests. Based on the results, they gave me a list of careers that might be suitable and told me how to research them. I did, and this is what I thought I'd like best.

This is a great answer that demonstrates this candidate's ability to go about making life-altering decisions in a methodical fashion.

Never Say: "My parents had a friend in the field and she thought I'd be good at this." That is the wrong way to make a career choice. It may make the interviewer wonder how this person will make other decisions.

Chapter 4

Discussing Your Skills and Abilities

YOUR SKILLS—THAT'S WHAT they pay you the big bucks for. Well, maybe not the big bucks, but it is why they pay you anything at all. Who you are as a person will help an employer decide if you have the characteristics that make you a good fit for his company. To fit into a particular job, you'll also need a certain set of skills. Your skills represent your ability to do the job at hand.

Hard Skills Versus Soft Skills

Skills can be divided into two categories: hard skills and soft skills. Hard skills are the technical skills that define your job. Soft skills are less tangible. They begin with how you present yourself in your first encounter with your prospective employer, whether it is a phone call or a sit-down interview. Your prospective employer will want to know that you will fit into the work environment at her company and that you are able to handle the demands that will be placed upon you.

Hard Skills

Simply put, a baker must know how to bake, an accountant must know how to balance the books, a nurse must know how to care for patients, and a teacher must know how to teach. Of course, these basic skills can be broken down into more specific hard skills. For example, an accountant might be skilled in particular areas—specifically, accounts receivable, accounts payable, auditing, taxation, and payroll.

 Fact

> Hard skills are usually skills you learned in school or through some other formal training or prior work experience. You will typically choose a job based on the hard skills you possess, but some employers are willing to let you pick them up on the job.

What you do at work can vary greatly from your formal job description. In addition to your regular job duties, you may be required to write, make presentations, use a computer, or do research. These are also hard skills, but they are not necessarily part of your "official" job description. Nevertheless, you will be required to be proficient in these skills and your prospective employer will want you to prove this to him in the job interview by drawing on specific examples of how you have used your skills.

Soft Skills

Soft skills are the skills you must have in order to excel at work in general. These skills vary greatly. They aren't specific to any occupation, but instead are the things that enhance your performance regardless of what your actual job is. Examples of these soft skills include decision-making, time management, delegating, multitasking, and problem solving.

Remember, when the job interviewer asks whether you have a particular skill, she doesn't want a simple yes or no answer. She wants to know how you obtained the skill, how you've used the skill, and how you plan to use it to benefit her company.

Essential

When you prepare for a job interview, make a list of all your soft skills and all your hard skills. Think of specific examples of when you've had to use each of them, especially those that are most relevant to the job for which you are interviewing.

Skills You Haven't Used Professionally

You may be concerned if you have a particular skill, but you haven't actually used it on the job. You may have learned the skill in school and never used it at work. If this is the case, can you think of a time you used that skill for an extracurricular activity or in another situation? Perhaps you used your fundraising skills to raise money for an organization for which you volunteer or your organizational skills to plan an event.

 Fact

People develop skills in a variety of ways that are unrelated to paid employment. You may have learned a new skill when you participated in a school club or organization. You may use certain skills in running your household or in your volunteer work.

When discussing skills you've picked up through volunteer work or some other unpaid experience, talk about the skill as if you used it on a job. Highlight how your skills benefited the organization with which you were involved. For example, if you raised funds for an organization, give dollar amounts; if you organized an event, state how many people attended it. If you haven't actually used a skill in a real-life situation, you can still lay claim to it. Come up with an example of how you would use that skill to benefit your prospective employer.

Questions and Answers

Q How well do you think you perform as a manager?

A I've never officially had the title "manager," but I've often had to act as manager when my boss is out of the office. He's always been very pleased with the job I've done.

This candidate doesn't let the fact that she's never actually had the title of manager stop her from explaining why she can do the job. She found some managerial experience from which she was able to draw. Even supervising a small project would have sufficed.

Never Say: "Well, since I've never been a manager, I don't know." If you've had some managerial experience, even if it was just supervising a single project, you should talk about that. If you've had no managerial experience, then you can talk about it hypothetically.

Q How are your presentation skills? How do you prepare for presentations?

A I didn't always like making presentations, but since I had to make a lot of them in my last two jobs, I've gotten very good at it. I do a lot of research before any presentation. I try to find out as much as possible about the client, the market they are trying to reach, their competitors, and the industry. Sometimes, if the budget allows for it, I hire an expert to help me with the research.

This candidate answered honestly. He knows it's not that unusual to dislike presentations, so he's not afraid to admit that. It also gives him the opportunity to show off his experience and how it has gotten him over his fear. In addition, he knows the importance of having good information and knows what resources he needs to use to get it.

Never Say: "I love making presentations. I only have one real problem; if I'm too prepared, my presentation sounds scripted." This is not a well-thought-out answer. This candidate would have benefited from a little preparation to get him through the interview.

Q You haven't worked in this field before. What makes you think you'd be good at this?

A I am very organized, I work well on a team, and I have very good communication skills. Although I haven't worked in this particular field before, I know these skills will make me a valuable employee.

This applicant doesn't let the fact that she's new to this field stop her from showing the interviewer why he should hire her. She has some very desirable skills for this and any field, which she makes a point of letting the interviewer know.

Never Say: "I haven't worked in this field before, but I'm a fast learner." This candidate makes the mistake of dwelling on her lack of experience in this particular field instead of on her strengths.

Q Have you ever been in a situation where the majority disagrees with you? What did you do?

A I haven't been in that situation, but here's what I would do if I were: first I would listen to why the majority felt the way they did. Then I'd have to decide whether I needed to reconsider my position. If I still felt strongly about it after hearing their side, I would try to persuade them to come over to mine.

This candidate knew better than to dismiss the question just because he couldn't draw on his experience to answer it. Rather than make something up, he tells the interviewer what he would do if he were in that situation. His answer shows that he is flexible enough to try to see things differently, but strong enough in his convictions to not automatically go with the crowd.

Never Say: "We were designing our new brochure and I thought yellow and purple would look great. Everyone else wanted to go with burgundy and blue. Since I had the most seniority, they had to do it my way." Flexible? No. A bully? Maybe.

Q Please describe your work in the military.

A As an Army finance specialist, I audited financial records, disbursed cash and checks, and recorded details of financial transactions using standard forms.

This job candidate, an Army veteran, clearly states what her military work involved. Since military job descriptions are often different than civilian job descriptions, it was not only important for her to state what her title was, but to also describe her duties.

Never Say: "I was a finance specialist." This isn't descriptive enough, particularly since the title may differ from the actual job description.

Q How are you at delegating?

A I have such a high level of trust in my staff members that delegating to them is easy. I know each person's strengths and weaknesses, so I can easily decide who can handle certain jobs and duties. I try to give people projects that challenge them but won't defeat them.

This candidate is obviously a good manager. He puts a lot of thought into how to delegate responsibilities and makes a point of knowing his staff very well.

Never Say: "I'm good at delegating. I don't want to do all the work myself." This guy just sounds lazy.

Q Tell me about a crisis you encountered at work and how you handled it.

A Last year a virus was causing our computers to send out thousands of e-mail messages to our clients. We were being inundated with angry phone calls before we even knew what was going on. Our technical support person was on vacation, so I made a few phone calls and found someone to fix the problem. Then, once she removed the virus from our system, I drafted an apology that was sent out by e-mail to our clients.

This answer is good because the candidate clearly describes the problem and gives specifics on how he solved it. In addition, the crisis is one that could have caused his company to lose clients, something that would strike fear into the hearts of most employers, including the one interviewing him.

Never Say: "My assistant called in sick right before I was leaving on vacation. I was counting on her to run some errands for me. Since she wasn't there I had to get one of the interns to do it." This candidate is resourceful, but he shouldn't have had anyone running his errands on company time.

Q How do you manage your time?

A I prioritize my work. I figure out what needs to get done first, next, and so on. Then I calculate how much time I will need to spend on each activity or project. I set a schedule for myself and get going.

This applicant has a plan. He knows how to prioritize and apportion the proper amount of time to each activity.

Never Say: "I get to work early and stay late to get everything done." This answer doesn't show that the applicant can manage his time well. Rather, he can get everything done as long as he works long hours, which could cost the employer in overtime.

Q How do you solve problems?

A First I assess the problem. Then I figure out what I need to do to solve it. For example, last month we were hosting a conference. Our receptionist, who was supposed to greet attendees, called in sick. With the conference scheduled to start in an hour we had to do something fast. I quickly went through a list of employees who might be able to handle hosting duties but found that each was involved in some other aspect of the conference. I got my boss's approval to call my contact at a local temp agency, and we had a replacement host shortly.

Not only does this applicant discuss how she solves problems, she gives a real-life example.

Never Say: "If you do your job well, you shouldn't have any problems to solve." This candidate is in a state of denial. Problems always pop up and she has shown that she will have no idea how to deal with them when they do.

Q We use PQR Write to lay out our brochures. Do you know how to use it?

A I use a program that is very similar to that. I also have a friend who uses PQR and I'm sure she'd be happy to give me a crash course. I know I can learn it by the time I start work.

There are so many software programs out there, it would be impossible to know how to use all of them. This candidate knew better than to lie about his experience and instead told his prospective employer how he would get the skills he needs. Notice how he says he'll know the program by the time "I start work," not "if I get this job."

Never Say: "No, I only feel comfortable with Super Page. Couldn't I just keep using that?"

Q Are you computer literate?

A I'm proficient in several programs, including WordRight, Bottom Line, and Quick Pages.

Instead of just saying she is computer literate, this candidate goes beyond that and discusses which software programs she knows how to use. The programs she chooses to highlight are those that are relevant to the job for which she's applying.

Never Say: "I know how to go online and I can use a word processor." This candidate should be more specific, making a point of mentioning programs that are specific to his field.

Q We handle a large volume of tax returns here. How has your experience prepared you for this?

A During college, I participated in the IRS's Volunteer Income Tax Assistance program. For two nights a week from February through April, I spent a few hours preparing individual tax returns in a public library near my college. I prepared about five returns each evening.

This job candidate, although he doesn't have professional experience, is able to demonstrate his skills through his volunteer experience. He speaks about the number of tax returns he processed, demonstrating that he can work efficiently.

Never Say: "I do a few returns each year but I'm sure I'll be able to handle the volume." Even if this candidate can't demonstrate that he has practical experience preparing a large volume of tax returns, he should find some past experience that proves to the interviewer he can handle a large volume of work.

Q Have you ever had to juggle two or more projects at the same time?

A That happened all the time on my last job. Several months ago, I was in the midst of working on one huge project for one of my bosses, when my other boss came to me with another project that needed to be completed in two days. After evaluating the second project, I realized I could complete it in one day. Since I still had about a week before the deadline for the first project, I decided to get started on the second one. I completed it by the end of the next day and went back to my first project.

The interviewer asked for an example and this candidate gave one. She demonstrates how her ability to prioritize helped her.

Never Say: "I can't think of any right now. Can I get back to you on that one?" The interviewee should have prepared for this in advance.

Q What does your desk look like?

A I try to keep it organized, which is not always an easy feat with the volume of work that comes across it. I find that if I know where everything is I can work much more efficiently.

This is a vague question, but this interviewee has quickly figured out that the interviewer wants to know how well-organized he is. He gives a realistic answer. He knows the importance of having an organized work area, but he also knows that it's sometimes difficult to keep it that way, especially when you're very busy.

Never Say: "It's brown and made of wood." This isn't what the interviewer wanted to know.

Q We need someone with very strong auditing skills. Do you qualify?

A Yes, I do. As a staff accountant at Crabgrass and Weed, I regularly performed audits of our clients' financial records. I examined financial source documents to make sure procedures were followed correctly and generated adjusting journal entries as needed. I also prepared final reports for our clients.

The interviewee specifically states how her experience has prepared her for this position.

Never Say: "Yes, I do. I had some auditing responsibilities on my last job." This applicant has the necessary skills, but she needs to elaborate on them.

Q How do you take direction?

A I think the ability to listen is one of the most important skills anyone should have. I always make sure to pay attention to what my supervisor is saying and then ask any questions I have. I find out when the project must be completed and if there are any special issues I must be attentive to.

This candidate demonstrates that he has no problem taking direction from his superiors, or for that matter, following those directions.

Never Say: "Why should that matter? Won't I be in charge?" Even if this person is applying for a high-level position, he will still have to answer to someone, unless he plans to buy the company.

Q As assistant to the director of human resources, employees will come to you if they feel their supervisor has discriminated against them in some way. How will you handle these complaints?

A As an HR professional I know the importance of being well versed in the laws that affect the workplace. First, I will interview the employee, asking for an explanation of exactly what happened. Then, I'll interview the supervisor and get her side of the story.

This candidate will take a balanced look at the situation. He will evaluate it using his knowledge of employment law and then try to solve the problem.

Never Say: "I'd refer it to our company's legal counsel." This applicant needs to show he knows how to deal with issues that regularly occur before dumping them in someone else's lap.

Q What skills can you bring to our school?

A As you can see from my resume, I've been a teacher at the Parkside School for five years. I've taught second and third grades. I form strong relationships with my students. They trust me, as do their parents. Many view me as a strict teacher, and in fact, I am an excellent classroom manager. My students know what I expect of them and are generally very cooperative. I am a skilled communicator. I structure my lessons so that I reach all my students. My classes always perform well on statewide exams.

This applicant knows what skills make a successful teacher and she has shown that she possesses them all.

Never Say: "I love kids and I'm a good teacher." This candidate needs to do more than state the obvious.

Q As principal, the most frequent complaint I hear from parents is about teachers who don't maintain good communications with them. What have you done as a teacher to help maintain communication with parents of your students?

A First of all, parents can reach me by e-mail, by sending in a note, or by telephone. If I am not able to respond immediately, I always get back to them before the end of the day. I encourage parents to come to the classroom to read to the children. I send home a "Dear Parents" letter every two weeks explaining what we've covered in the classroom during the prior two weeks and what we will be covering during the upcoming weeks.

This job candidate talks about what he is currently doing to maintain good communications with parents. Not only does he communicate with parents when he has an issue to discuss, he also keeps the lines of communication open.

Never Say: "When there's a problem, I contact the parents immediately." The principal wants to know how this teacher communicates regularly, not only if there's something that needs to be discussed.

Q Have you ever done therapy with a group before?

A Yes, I have. When I worked at the University, I organized a support group for students coping with panic attacks. I met with them once a week. I also took over a support group for families of cancer patients when I worked at Old Hills Hospital.

This job candidate has given two examples that demonstrate her skills, even highlighting a time that she not only worked with a group but organized one.

Never Say: "Yes, I have." Remember, you need to back this up with an example.

Q You have many of the skills we're looking for. However, we also need someone with very strong sales skills. I don't see anything on your resume that indicates you have that kind of experience.

A Yes, it's true that I don't have any formal experience in sales. I do have some informal experience, however. I ran the book fair at my son's school for the past few years and raised $3,000. I also sold jewelry that a friend made. We rented tables at craft fairs all over the region and sold about twenty pieces at each one. Even after covering the price of the table and supplies and paying me, she made a decent profit.

While a candidate can't make up experience, he should draw on unpaid or volunteer experience that demonstrates his skills. He gives very specific examples.

Never Say: "No, I don't have any sales experience, but I can learn." This candidate should try to find some past experience that demonstrates his skills. If he truly has no sales experience, he might consider the qualities that make a good salesperson and find a way to demonstrate that he has those qualities.

Q We expect the executive director to handle a lot of fundraising. Do you have any experience with that?

A Yes, I do. I spearheaded a campaign that raised more than $10,000 for a small library for our members. I also run an annual campaign to raise money for our after-school center. Over the last five years, we've increased donations by about 6 percent each year.

This candidate quantifies her accomplishments. It's one way of saying "here's what I did for my current employer and this is what I can do for you."

Never Say: "I've done some fundraising on my job." This candidate needs to be more specific.

Q Why should we hire you to be senior manager of our technical support department? You don't have any experience in technical support.

A While I don't have any experience in technical support, I do have six years of experience in customer service and management. I know how important it is to provide a good experience for customers. It builds loyalty, which will keep them coming back. I've managed customer service departments with staffs that ranged from fifteen to 100 employees.

Although this candidate's experience is not in technical support, he has managed departments that deal with consumer issues. He explains how that experience qualifies him for this position.

Never Say: "I use computers all the time, so I know how to answer the questions we would get." Computer skills do not qualify this applicant for a managerial position.

Q What is your management style?

A I'm a hands-on manager. I dive right in and work alongside my employees. This not only sets a good example for them, but also helps keep me aware of everyone's strengths and weaknesses.

This interviewee knows how to keep people motivated. She provides a reason for having chosen that style.

Never Say: "I'm very strict. I say how and when things get done." Ruling with an iron fist does not lead to a satisfied staff.

Q Are you good at doing research?

A I haven't done a great deal of research at work, but I do a lot of it on my own. Before I make any major purchases, take any medication, or go on vacation, I do a lot of research. I'm very good at it. The librarians at my local library are a great resource, so I make sure to go to them when I need help.

It would have been nice if this job candidate could have drawn on work experience to highlight his research skills, but since he couldn't, he did the next best thing. He gave examples of what kind of research he has done and explains how he does it.

Never Say: "I guess so. I like using the Net." An avid Internet user does not necessarily make a good researcher.

Q As you know, this is a new programming director position. We're thinking about having the person in this

position also handle promoting our programs. Is that something you can handle?

A My primary responsibility as program director at the Art Council was program development. However, we had a very small staff, so I was usually responsible for promotion as well. I wrote press releases, designed print ads, and compiled mailing lists. This would be a great way to utilize my skills.

While highlighting her primary skill, program development, this applicant also draws upon some of her secondary responsibilities to explain why this job is a good fit.

Never Say: "I would be thrilled to be doing publicity. That was my favorite part of my last job." The interviewer said that publicity *might* be part of this job. If it turned out not to be, would this candidate be disappointed and quit?

Q How do you think others rate you as a supervisor?

A Turnover in my department since I was promoted to supervisor five years ago has decreased from 30 percent to 10 percent. The reason, I believe, is that I treat those who work under me fairly. When a big deadline is coming up, I'm right there working late with them and not heading out the door at 5 P.M. I've had employees tell me they appreciate that.

This candidate knows that saying he's highly regarded as a supervisor isn't enough. He needs to back up his claim, which he does by telling his prospective employer how much turnover in his department decreased since he's been there. He goes on to tell the interviewer why he believes this is so.

Never Say: "They think I'm a good supervisor. They never complain and they do what I tell them to do." There's more to being a good supervisor than this.

Q What skills can you bring to the pediatric unit at St. Ernestine?

A I worked with children for about eight years as an assistant nursery school teacher before going back to school to become a nurse. When I began nursing school, I knew I wanted to specialize in pediatrics. I relate well to children and they relate well to me. I am a compassionate nurse as well as a skilled one. I offer patients the comfort they need when they are terrified of being in the hospital.

This answer demonstrates the candidate's experience working with children as well as his nursing skills.

Never Say: "I've spent four years training to be a nurse." This isn't enough information.

Q I see from your resume this isn't your first job working in a medical office. What skills did you pick up on your two previous jobs that you think would help you on this job?

A When you described the job to me, you said you needed someone who was good with patients. You also said you wanted someone who knows a lot about the different insurance plans. My primary responsibility at both these jobs was billing. I had to deal with insurance companies every day. I found that if I learned how each one worked, it was a lot easier for the doctors in my practice to get paid and for patients to get reimbursed. I also worked at the reception desk at these jobs. Many patients who came in were clearly anxious. I was happy to be able to calm them down and hopefully offer some reassurance.

This candidate listened to what the employer said and was able to clearly state how her skills would fill this medical practice's needs.

Never Say: "You wanted someone who is good with patients and insurance. That would be me." This candidate needs to elaborate.

Q Please discuss a project you supervised.

A I managed the expansion project at the shopping mall in Green-haven. It involved increasing the size of the mall by 20 percent. I supervised a staff of fifty-five project team professionals. We completed the project within our budget.

By giving details about this project, including specific numbers, this interviewer demonstrates the type of work of which he's capable.

Never Say: "I supervised a mall expansion right outside the city. It went well." This answer is too vague.

Q What traits will a person need in order to become successful? Do you have these traits?

A To be successful, a person needs excellent organization and time management skills. She has to get along well with her boss, coworkers, and clients. She must always be willing to learn new skills. Yes, I have all these traits.

This interviewee has chosen to discuss some very valuable skills—organization, time management, willingness to learn, and getting along with others.

Never Say: "A person must be good at office politics. I've had lots of experience with that, and I'm very good at it." Knowing how to play the game may help you be successful, but your success may not be based on any real skills.

Chapter 5

Highlighting Your Accomplishments

WHEN YOU GO in for a job interview, the prospective employer will be very interested in learning about your accomplishments as well as your personality and skills. Your accomplishments give him insight into what you are capable of doing for him and his company. An accomplishment, also known as an achievement, can be defined as something that you successfully completed as a direct result of your efforts.

Listing Your Accomplishments

Prepare a list of your accomplishments prior to your job interview. The accomplishments you choose to highlight should demonstrate your skills and abilities. Remember to use examples of things that came about as a direct result of your efforts. They shouldn't be things that happened to you, like raises or promotions, but rather things you made happen. That's not to say you shouldn't mention that your employer promoted you or rewarded you in some other way because of something you accomplished—you should talk about that. Before you do, however, discuss the accomplishment that led to your reward and the role you played in making your accomplishment come about.

The accomplishments you include on your list should be realistic and verifiable. Never stretch the truth—not even a little bit—on a job interview. The interviewer might be suspicious of something that sounds too good to be true and decide to check up on it. If she tries to verify something you told her and cannot, it will certainly reflect poorly on you. Telling a lie is much worse than not having a long list of accomplishments.

When possible, quantify your accomplishments. Use actual numbers or percentages when you are discussing anything that can be expressed in quantifiable terms, such as increases in profits or decreases in costs. Being able to say you increased sales by 20 percent or cut your department's costs by 35 percent is much better than saying "I increased sales a lot" or "I cut costs greatly."

 Fact

Consider keeping a career journal to record all of your achievements and the steps you took to achieve your goals. This will help you be specific on future job interviews. Listing accomplishments as they occur is easier than trying to think back and recall them.

When deciding which achievements to discuss on an interview, always remember to choose the ones that best demonstrate your ability to do the job for which you are interviewing. Highlight skills you think the prospective employer is looking for in a new employee.

Discussing Your Accomplishments

You will have many opportunities to talk about your accomplishments throughout a job interview. The prospective employer will, of course, ask you direct questions about your accomplishments. You can also impress the interviewer with additional accomplishments if you answer his questions about your skills by discussing how a particular skill helped you achieve something.

A prospective employer is likely to ask you questions about your goals, both work-related and personal. Your goals are merely accomplishments waiting to happen. Discuss goals you have already reached and those you are moving toward reaching. Talk about the steps you took, or are taking, to do so.

This is your time to brag about what you have done and what you can do. People are often quite hesitant to speak highly of themselves. They are under the impression that being boastful is obnoxious. This may, in fact, be true in our private lives. But the job interview is not the time for modesty. You must sell yourself, and to do so you have to show off.

Alert

You may be asked about your personal goals as well as your professional ones. Even when discussing personal goals and achievements, make sure they highlight an ability related to work; for example, perseverance or organizational skills.

Questions and Answers

Q Can you tell me about your greatest accomplishment at work?

A I'm particularly proud of the mentoring program I started about five years ago. I noticed that new employees were having trouble getting acclimated to the company, causing a very high turnover rate during the first year of employment. I developed a program that allowed us to assign each new employee to an employee who had been with the company for at least three years. This allowed new hires to make a smoother transition. Now, 90 percent of new employees are still with us after their one-year anniversaries, up from 50 percent before we started the mentorship program.

The interviewee provides a specific example in response to this question. She also highlights the fact that she took initiative in developing it—she saw a problem and found a solution. Notice that she uses actual numbers to illustrate the result of her efforts.

Never Say: "I was promoted to assistant director of human resources." While it is important to share this information, this interviewee doesn't indicate what led to that promotion.

Q How did you progress at your last job?

A I was hired as a sales associate by K. R. Nickel Stores seven years ago. I became assistant manager of the girls' clothing department two years later. My boss said she never saw a young associate work as hard as I did. After two more years I was promoted to manager of that department.

This candidate simply describes his ascent up the corporate ladder, giving details, as he was asked to do.

Never Say: "I started as a sales associate and seven years later I'm manager of girls' clothing." This interviewee must talk about how he got from point A to point C.

Q How do you feel about the way your career has progressed so far?

A I'm pleased with how my career has progressed. When I graduated from college, I was hired to work as a trainee at Rogers, Inc., a small advertising agency. Being a trainee meant I answered the phones and made coffee. I took the initiative and asked for additional work. That gave me the opportunity to prove myself, and I was promoted to assistant account executive after eight months. After two years in that position, during which I worked on several successful ad campaigns, I was promoted to account executive. I'm proud of my work there, but it's time for a position with more responsibility.

This candidate takes the time to explain how her career has progressed since her graduation from college. She also makes sure to point out how she contributed to her firm's success.

Never Say: "I am very happy with it. I started off answering phones and now look where I am." Don't assume the interviewer knows where you are right now or how you got there.

Q Why do you think you've been successful in your career so far?

A I've been successful so far because I've always worked very hard and I've always been willing to accept any challenges that are offered to me. Actually, I usually seek them out. I have excellent time management skills that have allowed me to complete projects on time.

This interviewee hasn't relied on luck to achieve success. He has used his skills and motivation to get where he wants to be.

Never Say: "I've always been in the right place at the right time." This candidate doesn't seem to think he had anything to do with his own success. If he doesn't believe it, who will?

Q Which of your accomplishments has given you the most satisfaction?

A Last year I initiated a program that sent our executives into schools to work with the Young Entrepreneur Program. We sent teams into two area high schools to help the students learn how to run their own businesses. Our executives taught them how to write a business plan, design an ad campaign, make sales calls, and deal with clients. We ended up hiring some of the kids as interns, which worked out really well.

The accomplishment this job candidate has chosen to highlight involves giving back to the community, which is certainly admirable. While it doesn't directly benefit the company in terms of sales or earnings, participation in a program such as the one she describes is good for a company's public image.

Never Say: "My boss made me Senior Community Liaison. Finally having a title has been great." This candidate needs to focus on something she did in order to deserve that title.

 **Question**

What should I do if I'm a recent college graduate without many work-related accomplishments?
If you don't have much work experience, draw upon your experiences as a student. Look at what you achieved while you were in college, either in your classes or through extracurricular activities.

Q Do you consider your progress on your current job indicative of your ability?

A Yes, I do. I was promoted twice on my current job. I was hired as a marketing trainee. After about a year I was promoted to associate account executive, and then after two years I was promoted to account executive. My promotions came about because I proved that I could successfully meet deadlines, win the confidence of clients, and solve problems.

This candidate discusses how and why she was promoted.

Never Say: "Yes." This answer lacks specifics.

Q Describe how you accomplished a work-related goal.

A When I started working for Daylight Publications, I discovered that I had inherited a huge file cabinet full of photographs. We used photographs in our magazine but usually wound up purchasing stock photos, because our own collection was so disorganized it was impossible to find anything. I designed a filing system and set about putting things in order. I set aside 15 minutes each day and was able to work my way through the whole collection in about seven months.

This answer demonstrates how the interviewee took the initiative to set a goal in order to save her employer money. She then talks about how she went about reaching that goal by using her organization and time management skills.

Never Say: "I wanted to make $50,000 per year by the time I was twenty-six. I switched jobs a few times and was able to do it." This in no way demonstrates any job-related skills the interviewee has.

Q Can you describe how you accomplished a personal goal?

A I wrote a short story and my goal was to get it published. I went to the library and researched which magazines accepted short-story submissions. Then I sent my story to those publications that published stories in the same genre as mine. My story was accepted by one of them and was published a little over a year ago.

This candidate talks about the steps he took to reach his personal goal. While the goal isn't related to the job for which he is applying, he talks about his ability to do research, a skill he knows this prospective employer will value.

Never Say: "I won a hot dog-eating contest. I trained for about six months." This answer does not demonstrate any skills that are needed in the workplace.

Q Tell me how you were of value to your previous employer.

A My previous employer valued my ability to deal with difficult clients. Whenever we had a client who was very demanding, my boss would ask me to be the one to work with her. He said he knew I was so levelheaded that I would always stay calm, even when a client was really trying my patience.

By giving this answer the candidate not only says why she thinks her boss values her, she talks about it from her boss's perspective. She presents a skill that this employer will appreciate as well.

Never Say: "I always showed up on time." Showing up on time is expected and doesn't set this candidate apart from any other.

Q Have you ever had to take over an assignment at the last minute?

A I've had to do that more than once—actually several times. The most recent time was when a colleague was scheduled to attend a meeting out of town and came down with the flu two days before he was supposed to leave. My boss asked me if I could attend the meeting and make the presentation my colleague was supposed to make. I had two days to learn everything about the project. I went over pages and pages of notes and put together a presentation of my own, incorporating input from my colleague, who I spoke to on the phone several times a day.

Not only does this interviewee say she has taken over an assignment at the last minute, she talks about a specific case. She shows how she stepped in and learned what she needed to learn in order to make a successful presentation.

Never Say: "Yes, it has happened." She should give an example.

Q Have you ever received formal recognition for something you accomplished?

A Yes. I won Salesperson of the Month four times when I was working for Ace Stereo. Those with the largest increase in sales over the previous month were rewarded in this way. I believe I had increased my sales by 15 to 20 percent each time.

This candidate chose to discuss being rewarded for something that would be valued by any company—high sales volume. He gives actual numbers to quantify his answer.

Never Say: "I won best dressed at the annual holiday party." Unless this is a candidate for a fashion consulting position, this answer doesn't highlight any skills that will impress the employer.

Q What has been your greatest accomplishment as part of a team?

A I worked on a team that developed a program for children who were going home to an empty house after school because their parents worked. We had volunteers who would help the kids with their homework and give them time to just burn off energy after sitting in a classroom all day. By the time we actually opened the center, we had seventy-five children enrolled. That told us we were providing a service that was clearly needed.

This candidate describes in detail the project she considers the greatest accomplishment she achieved as part of a team. She talks about what was needed, what they did to fill that need, and what the end result was.

Never Say: "I never feel like I accomplish that much on a team." This candidate just admitted she's not a team player. It was a bad idea to do that. The interviewer probably asked the question because working on a team is probably typical of the position for which he is hiring.

Q Name the two work-related accomplishments of which you are proudest.

A I converted a manual payroll system to a computerized system, which cut down the amount of time we spend on payroll each week. I wrote a manual that explained all bookkeeping department procedures in our company. New employees receive a copy of this manual, which helps them learn their job faster.

Each of the accomplishments this candidate discusses has had a positive result on the company and highlights his many skills.

Never Say: "I received a good performance review every year. I was promoted to a supervisory position after just two years." While these are definitely positive things and a reflection of this candidate's ability to do a good job, they really don't address how his accomplishments affected the company. They also don't explain how he earned his good reviews and promotion.

Q Tell me about the personal accomplishment that you are the proudest of.

A Last year I ran a marathon for the first time. I've been a runner for years, but I never ran more than four miles at a time. I began training four months before the big day. It was hard, but I kept going and I ended up finishing in just over four hours, which I've heard is pretty good for a first-time marathoner.

By discussing running a marathon, this candidate demonstrates that she will work hard to reach her goals. She also shows that she is not afraid of a challenge, something her prospective employer should appreciate.

Never Say: "I bought my first house." Without an explanation of how she reached this goal, this candidate doesn't show off any strengths when she gives this example.

Q If I asked your current employer to tell us about your accomplishments, what do you think he would say?

A He would probably talk about the time he asked me to present a new marketing campaign to one of our more difficult clients. I spent over a week preparing for that presentation. Since I knew this client was hard to please, I had to make sure I anticipated every objection she might have. She actually loved the presentation and the campaign increased her company's sales by 50 percent.

This question gives the candidate a chance to talk about an accomplishment he is proud of. He talks about anticipating possible difficulties, as well as the end result, an increase in sales.

Never Say: "I doubt my boss recognized any of my accomplishments. If he did, he certainly didn't tell me." This candidate breaks one of the cardinal rules of job interviewing—never speak negatively about a former boss.

Q If I asked a college professor about one of your accomplishments, what would he or she say?

A I worked on a major research project under the supervision of my psychology professor. We collected data over the course of a year, and we analyzed it and wrote up the results as an article that we submitted to the *Journal of Kangaroo Psychology.* It was accepted and it was published a month before I graduated.

This candidate chose to talk about something that had a tangible result—publication of an article in a professional journal.

Never Say: "I got an A in a class that was very difficult." Even though this may have been a great personal achievement for this interviewee, it is probably not something a professor would recognize as a great achievement.

Q What does success mean to you?

A I feel I am successful when I do the best job I can possibly do, such as complete a project on time and under budget, and meet or go beyond my own expectations or those of my boss or my client. I also want to achieve the desired result, whether it is to make a profit or reduce a loss for my employer.

This candidate defines success by what he can accomplish for his employer rather than what he can accomplish for himself.

Never Say: "Success to me is making a six-figure salary."

Q Have you ever had to overcome a major obstacle? How did you do it?

A Yes, I did. My family couldn't afford to pay for college. I applied for as much financial aid as possible, but I still had to work to pay for whatever that didn't cover. I worked after classes every day and on the weekends, too. In the end, in addition to a college degree, I also had some valuable work experience under my belt.

The story this candidate tells demonstrates that she can set a goal—getting a college degree—and reach it through hard work. She even points out that, because of her need to overcome this obstacle, she now has valuable work experience.

Never Say: "I've been very lucky. I really haven't had any obstacles to overcome." Luck isn't what is going to get this candidate hired.

She needs to demonstrate perseverance and therefore should try to find some obstacle to speak about.

Q What accomplishments have you made so far in reaching your long-range goals?

A My long-range goal is to be a school principal. I've been teaching for ten years, first at PS 118 and then at PS 114. After five years of teaching second grade at PS 114, I was asked to be grade leader. My experience working with other faculty members and developing new programs for students has prepared me for the position of assistant principal. I look forward to using my skills to work on some of the projects we discussed earlier.

This candidate has demonstrated how he has taken steps to reach his goal and plans to continue to do so. He also makes a point of talking about the contributions he plans to make in the job for which he's interviewing.

Never Say: "I want to be an assistant principal." Since this is the job that he's interviewing for, this answer doesn't show motivation to reach any goals beyond that.

Q What motivates you to go above and beyond the call of duty?

A Honestly, I don't have a sense of what is above and beyond the call of duty. It's not like I can just do enough to get by and then stop. When I work on a project, I do my very best, always.

This statement shows that this job candidate is truly a hard worker who cares about her work. It's more than just a job to her. She can't justify giving less than her best effort to any project entrusted to her.

Never Say: "Hopefully, if I go above and beyond the call of duty, I'll get recognition for my work." This candidate doesn't seem to be self-motivated since her rewards come from the outside.

Q What one thing do you think you've done very well on your last job?

A I think I was very successful in all aspects of my last job. I'm particularly proud of my work with new hires. I developed programs that helped integrate them into the company and this in turn helped our ability to retain them as employees.

Because the interviewer has asked for one thing this person has done well, he is forced to only talk about one thing. He explains why he is particularly proud of that one accomplishment and explains how his success benefited his employer. He also makes a point of saying that this isn't his only success.

Never Say: "I can't think of just one thing." If you are asked for one thing, you should be able to come up with something. If not, it appears that you can't think of *anything* you did well at your last job.

Q How has your employer rewarded your accomplishments?

A My employer initially rewarded me by trusting me enough to give me additional responsibility. This gave me a chance to really prove myself and I was ultimately rewarded with a big promotion.

This candidate discusses how at first her reward was simply being asked to do more. Did she object to that? No. It only gave her the opportunity to further prove herself so that she received the reward of a promotion.

Never Say: "Rewarded? He didn't reward anyone for anything. I guess he thought our paycheck was good enough." This interviewee shouldn't speak with such animosity about his employer.

Q You seem to have accomplished a lot in your current job. Do you know why you weren't promoted?

A I wasn't promoted because unfortunately there wasn't a position to promote me to. JFR was a very small family-owned firm. The boss's two sons held the top positions, which were right above my position.

The candidate explains why he couldn't move beyond his current position in spite of his accomplishments. He doesn't seem resentful, but rather accepts this fact.

Never Say: "Sure I do. One word—nepotism. The boss's sons hold all the good positions. It doesn't matter how hard you work. You aren't moving up." This candidate is clearly resentful of the way things are at his current job and makes the mistake of letting the interviewer know that.

Q Have you ever come up with new ways to solve a problem?

A Yes, I have. We had a problem with dismissal from our after-school program. Too many children were leaving at once, causing chaos in our parking lot. I developed a system for releasing children alphabetically so that parents could pick up siblings in different grades at the same time. If we had released children by grade, parents would have had to wait around for children who were in different grade levels. That would have added to the chaos.

The candidate states a specific problem and then discusses the steps she took to solve it. She even mentions how she anticipated and then prevented a potential problem.

Never Say: "I'm lucky. I haven't had to solve any problems." If this candidate hasn't had to solve any problems, how can she be expected to do so in the future?

Q Have you ever "saved the day" for your employer?

A Yes, I have. It was the afternoon before our company was hosting a big luncheon. We called the caterer to confirm some of the details, but his number had been disconnected. We found out he had gone out of business and didn't bother to let us know. I called some friends at other companies and got a list of caterers together, called them, and got someone to do the job. My boss couldn't believe I managed to hire someone on such short notice.

The interviewee, by giving this example, shows how her resourcefulness helped her solve her employer's problem.

Never Say: "I've saved many days for them. I always have to fix everyone else's mistakes." This answer, even if it is true, makes the interviewee seem arrogant.

Q Have you ever been asked to take on a project because of your unique skill or ability?

A Our senior developer regularly asks me to troubleshoot new programs. I've been very successful at figuring out why programs aren't working properly and I can usually do it pretty quickly, allowing the team to move forward.

This candidate chose to talk about a skill that will be as valuable to his prospective employer as it is to his current one.

Never Say: "I'm very good at planning parties, so when my boss's secretary was retiring she asked me to plan the party." This skill probably won't be very important to the prospective employer.

Q Have you ever done something that directly helped your employer either increase profits or decrease costs?

A I recently found a way to help my employer save money on office supplies. For years, they bought office supplies from the same place. It was several blocks away, so it was pretty convenient. I have found that shopping online is almost always less expensive than shopping in a store, so I did a little comparison shopping and I found an online source for our office supplies at a savings of 40 percent from what we were paying for the same items. Plus, the order is delivered to the office, which is even more convenient. As long as we order several items at once, delivery is free.

This interviewee's answer illustrates how he looks out for his employer's best interests.

Never Say: "I just go about doing my job. I guess that increases their profits, doesn't it?" This candidate needs to remember he's trying to sell himself to this employer. Instead of saying he'll "just do the job," he needs to show why he'd be great at it.

Q Have you ever been assigned a project you didn't think you'd be able to get through? If so, what happened?

A I've been assigned many projects that seemed difficult at first, but I refuse to think of any project as impossible. Before I begin any project, I think about how I'm going to tackle it. I come up with a plan and take it step by step. If I think I need help with a project, I ask for advice from those with more experience.

This candidate demonstrates that she will not be defeated by any project, yet she is not averse to asking for help when she needs it. She explains how she approaches all projects in a systematic fashion.

Never Say: "There isn't a project I can't get through." There's a difference between self-assurance and cockiness. Without explaining what she does in order to get through difficult projects, this candidate just sounds cocky.

Q It seems like you've accomplished a lot. I know everyone fails, at least occasionally. Tell me about something you failed at.

A When I was a freshman in college I decided to run for president of the management club. My opponent was in his junior year. I came up with what I thought and still think was a great platform. I campaigned vigorously. Unfortunately I lost the election. I'm pretty sure it was due to my lack of experience. I ran too early in my school career. Two years later I ran again and I won.

The applicant chooses to discuss a failure that isn't work-related and attributes it to her lack of experience rather than something she had control over.

Never Say: "I ran for president of the management club and lost." The applicant must give a more detailed answer. This one leaves the interviewer to wonder why the applicant lost the election.

Q Is there anything I've missed?

A Well, I did want to mention that I was honored by my organization's board of directors for developing a program that reached out to a large number of senior citizens in need of financial assistance. We now help just over 650 seniors each year.

The candidate uses this opportunity to bring to the interviewer's attention an accomplishment he didn't discuss previously.

Never Say: "No. I think you just about covered it all. Are we done?" This candidate sounds like he's in a hurry for the interview to be over. Since it is unlikely that everything has been covered, he may be missing a chance to discuss something that can work in his favor.

Chapter 6

Questions about Your Education

WHEN PROSPECTIVE EMPLOYERS interview recent graduates without much experience, they can learn a lot about them by asking questions about their school experience. Therefore, if you're interviewing for jobs straight out of school, you should be prepared to answer a lot of questions about your education. Even if you've been working for a few years, you may still be asked about your education, so it's important to have your answers ready.

How You Spent Your College Years

The interviewer will want to know about your performance as a student. As you know, the grades on a college transcript don't always tell the whole story. A failing grade may mean more than an inability in a particular subject and a high grade may mean more than great achievement.

The interviewer will want to know how you felt about particular subjects, which ones you found challenging, and which ones you thought were a piece of cake. She may ask which instructors you liked and why. All of this information lets her get a better look at who you are.

In addition to simple questions like "Where did you go to school?" and "What was your major?" the interviewer will likely ask you about activities you participated in outside the classroom. She will want to know about your involvement in extracurricular activities such as participation in on-campus clubs and organizations, work on student-run publications, and community service. All these activities contributed to your education and make up who you are today—and what you will bring to an employer. Think about your activities in terms of the skills they helped you develop. When you can't prove your worth by talking about your work experience, you must prove it by discussing what you did during your time in school.

Essential

When asked about extracurricular activities, you should think of each one as a job. What contributions did you make to a particular club? Can you quantify them? Did you help raise money for a charity? How much? Did you work for your school newspaper? How many hours a week did that involve? What were your successes and what were your failures?

Many students gain valuable work experience by doing an internship. If you did one, be prepared to discuss it in great detail. Even if you didn't get paid, you should consider it equivalent to a job. The interviewer will want to know what you did there, what you learned, and what contributions you made to the company or organization.

The prospective employer has something else on her agenda, too. She is interested in knowing why and how you made your choices over the last several years. For example, she wants to know how you chose what college to attend. She wants to find out how you decided on your major. Seeing how you made these very important choices offers her the opportunity to learn what your decision-making process is generally like.

Questions and Answers

Q I see you majored in English. Are you prepared for a job in marketing and sales?

A As an English major I had to do a large amount of reading and needed to retain all of the information. Reading and absorbing the literature on the products I'll be selling will be a snap. I believe college also prepared me to manage my time well. I do have hands-on experience in this field as well; I worked in various sales positions in order to put myself through school.

Notice that the interviewee doesn't make any excuses for wanting to work in a field outside his major. Instead, he talks about how his major qualifies him for this job. He also talks about the fact that he has sales experience.

Never Say: "I guess I could teach at a college with my English degree but then I'd have to get a PhD. I definitely don't want to do that." The interviewer knows what this applicant doesn't want to do, but she still doesn't know how the interviewee can transfer his skills to this field.

Q Why did you choose Adams University?

A Adams University has an accredited business school. It is ranked third in the nation. The university also has a great cross-country team and I wanted to try out for it.

This candidate put a lot of thought into choosing a college, implying that's how she makes all her decisions. She also uses this opportunity to brag about the quality of her education.

Never Say: "My best friend was going there." This applicant doesn't demonstrate that she puts a lot of thought into making important decisions.

Q I see you majored in marketing. What courses did you take outside your major?

A I took a few psych classes because I felt that knowing how people think would be to my advantage in marketing. I took some art classes because I really enjoy them. I also took writing courses, because I thought that was an important skill to have.

Instead of just giving a list of courses, this candidate talks about why she took them. She even explains how two of the subjects will help in her career.

Never Say: "I decided just to take extra courses in my major." While this candidate may think she's showing how much she knows about her field by having taken extra courses in it, she is actually showing that she's not well rounded.

 **Question**

What should I do if my major and my career choice are unrelated?
If you did not major in a subject that traditionally prepares people to work in the career field you are pursuing, you are going to have some explaining to do. Be ready to discuss how your major prepared you for this occupation even though they are seemingly unrelated to one another.

Q Did you have any teachers who influenced you?

A Yes, I did. It goes all the way back to junior high school. Mr. Danzer was my earth science teacher. He loved the subject and he loved teaching. I think both these things came across in his ability to teach. It showed me that if a person loves what he does, he's more likely to excel at it. That was good to know when it came time to choose a career.

This candidate answers the question with just enough information to satisfy the interviewer.

Never Say: "No." If you can't think of one single teacher, perhaps you can mention the qualities of several who had some sort of impact on you.

Q Why did you choose to major in philosophy?

A From a very early age I wanted to be a lawyer. When I started to do my research, I found out that undergraduates who want to go to law school should take a lot of liberal arts classes. During my freshman year, I took different courses in the school of liberal arts and sciences and I liked philosophy the best, so I decided to make it my concentration.

This applicant shows that she made an informed choice when choosing her major.

Never Say: "It looked interesting." While you should choose a major you think is interesting, that shouldn't be your only criteria.

Q What did you gain from attending college?

A I gained knowledge about this field. I was able to use what I learned in class on the internship I did last summer at the *Tallahassee Tribune.* College is where I learned to be independent. There wasn't anyone pushing me to complete assignments on time, so I had to learn how to manage my time well and stay organized.

This candidate talks about things he learned both in and out of the classroom. He includes technical skills as well as soft skills—time management and organization.

Never Say: "I got my degree." Isn't that on the resume? The candidate needs to come up with a more detailed answer than this one.

Q What was your favorite subject in high school? What was your favorite subject in college?

A English was my favorite subject in high school. I did a lot of writing in English. I liked working hard to put together a paper and then getting feedback in the form of a grade. My favorite classes in college were those in my major. I actually took only one marketing class before I declared marketing as my major. I found the subject matter so interesting that I started looking into it as a career choice.

This candidate explains why English was her favorite subject and in the process demonstrates her skill as a writer, which she knows will be an important part of her job. By stating that her major was her favorite subject in college, she shows her dedication to the field.

Never Say: "In high school I liked social studies. My favorite subject in college was sociology." This candidate needs to explain why these two subjects were her favorites.

Q What were your least favorite subjects in high school and college?

A My least favorite subject in high school was home economics. I helped with the housekeeping at home, and I didn't want to have to deal with it at school, too. I liked most of the classes I took in college. If I had to pick my least favorite I guess it would have to be biology. We had to dissect a fetal pig, and I had a problem doing that.

The candidate picked classes unrelated to the job for which he's applying. Also notice that he didn't say he disliked the classes because he found them difficult. Never imply that you don't like challenges.

Never Say: "My least favorite classes were geometry and matrix algebra. I couldn't get it. I guess math isn't my strong suit." This candidate makes the mistake of volunteering information about his weaknesses. While they may not be related to this job, they are challenges that defeated him.

☀ Alert

If the interviewer asks what your least favorite class was, pick one that is as unrelated as possible to your career field. If your least favorite class is one in which you received a failing grade, pick another one. Don't bring up a failing grade unless you are asked a direct question about it.

Q What extracurricular activities did you participate in?

A During my junior year of college, I was president of the psychology club. Then in my senior year I was editor of the yearbook. I wrote for both my high school and college newspapers, too.

This candidate highlights her leadership experience and writing skills, two very valuable attributes.

Never Say: "Academics took up all my time. I didn't have much time for anything else." This candidate may think she's showing what a dedicated student she was, but extracurricular activities enhance one's college experience. She should try to think of some valuable experience she had outside the classroom.

Q I see it took you four and a half years to graduate. Can you explain that?

A I had a difficult time adjusting during my freshman year. I wasn't quite ready for all the demands of college. I had to take a few classes over. During the summer between my freshman and sophomore years, I went to a few workshops to help me improve my study skills and my time management skills. By the time I was a sophomore, I was a much more serious student.

This candidate doesn't make excuses for his failings, but rather speaks about how he overcame them and how he succeeded in the end.

Never Say: "I had these really tough professors my freshman year. They wouldn't cut me any slack. When you're a freshman, you get stuck with teachers no one else wants." This candidate tries to blame everyone else for his failure.

Q Aside from coursework, what was the most enriching part of your college education?

A I was very involved on the programming committee. As a matter of fact, I was chair during my senior year. We were responsible for planning on-campus events for the student body. The goal was to hold events that were well attended and safe. That meant hiring entertainment that appealed to the majority of students and making sure campus security was present to enforce the rules. Our events were attended by between 60 and 70 percent of dormitory residents.

This applicant talks about her work on this committee as if it were a job. She highlights her leadership skills as well as other skills she drew upon in order to organize these events. This candidate also explains her goals and how she met them, giving actual numbers.

Never Say: "I was in some campus clubs and that was fun." This applicant needs to do a better job of explaining what those clubs were and how she participated in them.

Q I see you had an internship in this field. What did you learn from it?

A My internship at Carlson Corporate allowed me to get some hands-on experience in this field that I wouldn't have gotten in classes alone. I learned that jobs in this field are often stressful and long hours are usually required. On the other hand, I got to find out how wonderful it is when you're on a team that helps land a big account as a result of hard work.

This applicant speaks about what he gained from the internship and what he learned about the positive and negative aspects of working in the field.

Never Say: "Not a heck of a lot. I was just a glorified gopher." Even if all he did was deliver mail and make copies, this candidate should be able to come up with something he learned just from being exposed to the work environment of this particular field.

Q Why haven't you done any internships?

A I would have loved to have done an internship, but unfortunately I had to work my way through college. Most internships don't pay that well. However, as you can see from my resume, I made a point of finding work within this industry. Even though I was in the mailroom, I was still exposed to the field.

While internships are important, sometimes extenuating circumstances get in the way. This candidate has no choice but to be honest about that. However, she explains how she tried to make up for not being able to do an internship.

Never Say: "I won't work for free." This candidate sounds like she's only concerned with money and experience is worth nothing to her.

Q How did you spend your summers during college?

A I worked every summer to earn money for books and part of my tuition. I had this great job at a day camp. I started off as a counselor the summer before my senior year of high school, moved up to group leader the summer after I graduated, and then became assistant director.

This applicant takes the opportunity to show off a little. He stayed at the same job for several years and was promoted to a supervisory position.

Never Say: "I rested. School's hard." If he thinks school is hard, wait until he tries working—and he probably won't get two months off each year.

Essential

How you spent your summers while in school says a lot about you. Your experience may not be career-related, but it may give you the opportunity to highlight some positive qualities about yourself. If you were asked back to the same job summer after summer, your prospective employer can assume you earned that because of your job performance.

Q What grade did you receive in your favorite class?

A My favorite class was Intro to Journalism. It was actually pretty tough at first. Everything I handed in came back marked up in red ink. I must have gotten Ds on the first four assignments. There were a few times that my professor commented that I had found just the right words to describe an event, though, and I loved that feeling. I plugged away and kept trying harder. Fortunately, my professor gave us the opportunity to redo our work for a higher grade, and although it took a lot of extra work, ultimately I got an A in the class.

It's easy to like a class if you don't have to work hard for a good grade. This applicant explains why journalism was her favorite class despite it being difficult. Perseverance and the ability to meet a challenge are attributes all bosses value in their employees.

Never Say: "Intro to Journalism. I got an A." Without saying more than that, the interviewer is left to wonder whether the candidate liked that class simply because she got an A in it.

Q What grade did you receive in your least favorite class?

A My least favorite class was Art History. I know students who took the class with other professors, got a C, and loved it. I hated the class and got an A. I didn't learn anything. I just had to show up for every class and do little else.

Clearly this candidate doesn't mind working hard as long as he learns something. He isn't impressed with getting rewarded for "just showing up."

Never Say: "I got a D in it. It was Organic Chemistry, the hardest class I ever took. I can't believe how much I studied and all I ended up with was a D." Other than getting a bad grade, this candidate doesn't explain why this was his least favorite class. He just sounds like a sore loser.

Q Why did you decide to major in elementary education?

A When I was in high school, I took an assessment test to help me figure out what career I should go into. When I got my results, teaching was one of the occupations on the list, along with several others like psychology, social work, and nursing. When I started researching the occupations in more detail, I discovered that teaching was the one that appealed to me most.

This candidate put a lot of thought into choosing an occupation. This answer not only shows her dedication to teaching but also indicates that she makes decisions carefully.

Never Say: "I like children." While it's important to like children if you want to teach them, liking children doesn't necessarily mean you'll be good at teaching.

Q I see you transferred to Hamford University from Sannau County Community College. Why did you start your college education at a two-year school?

A I knew I wanted to earn a bachelor's degree. I also wanted to go to Hamford, but the cost of a four-year education there was extremely high. I decided to take my core classes at a community college to save money. I first checked to make sure Hamford would take my credits. Since Sannau is a very well-respected community college, I knew I would get a decent education there.

By giving this answer, the interviewee demonstrates that he is a very practical person. He spends money wisely but doesn't compromise his goals. He also doesn't do something without first investigating it.

Never Say: "I thought Sannau would be a good place to start my education." This doesn't explain what led to the transfer.

Q What would your professors say about you?

A My professors would say I always turned in high-quality work. They would say I contributed to classroom discussions by offering interesting comments and asking good questions. They would also say I was willing to help other students.

This candidate takes the opportunity to highlight some positive attributes.

Never Say: "They liked me." This interviewee doesn't take the opportunity to acknowledge her attributes. She should explain why her professors liked her.

Q What courses best prepared you for a job in this library?

A I took a course in research and bibliographic methods that provided me with the technical skills to do this job. The most important thing I learned in that class was that there is a resource available to answer almost all questions. I also took several classes in children's and young adult literature. I saw from the job description that the person who takes this position will also have to spend several hours a week in the children's department. Those courses have certainly helped prepare me for that.

This candidate not only lists some courses he took, but also explains how they will help him do the job should he be hired.

Never Say: "I took research and bibliographic methods and some children's lit classes. I think they'll be helpful." This candidate tells what classes he took but isn't specific about how they will enable him to do his job.

Q Are you planning to get your MBA?

A I would like to do that. I'm looking for a program with a schedule that won't interfere with work.

This interviewee knows that an MBA is highly valued in her field, but she anticipates that her potential employer might be concerned that her work schedule would be compromised if she pursues one. She heads off those fears.

Never Say: "I've already been accepted at NJU. The classes start at 5:45, so I'm hoping it will be okay if I cut out of here early three days a week." If the employer had a choice between this candidate and one who wouldn't need her schedule adjusted, who do you think he would choose? In addition, any discussion of that sort should wait until a job offer is received.

Q What elective accounting courses did you take?

A I took three auditing classes because I knew I wanted to work in public accounting. I also took an international accounting class. In this global economy I knew that would come in handy at some point in my career.

This candidate explains how she chose courses she would be able to use professionally.

Never Say: "I took a taxation class, an auditing class, and a corporate accounting class that all fit nicely into my schedule." This answer doesn't show that the candidate selected classes that would benefit her in her career.

Q Have you ever had a disagreement with a professor? How did you handle it?

A I disagreed about a grade I received once. I spent a lot of time researching and writing a paper for a history class. When I got the paper back with a B, I was very disappointed. After thinking about it for a day, I decided to talk to the professor. He asked me what grade I thought I deserved. I said I thought I had earned an A on the paper and explained why. He said he would read the paper over and re-grade it if he found my arguments were valid. The next day he told me he changed my grade to an A.

This applicant proves that she knows how to stand up for herself when there is something she feels strongly about. She demonstrates how she persuaded her teacher to change her grade by presenting her arguments in a calm manner after waiting a day to collect her thoughts.

Never Say: "I was very unhappy about a grade a professor gave me, but I didn't bother saying anything about it."

Q What was the most difficult assignment you had while in school?

A I took a creative writing class. It was one of several electives I could choose from outside my major. I had to write a poem. I discovered I'm not really good at that sort of thing.

This interviewee chose to discuss an assignment that was entirely unrelated to his major and to anything he would be expected to do at this job.

Never Say: "I hated writing papers, so any assignment that involved doing that was difficult." Since some writing is generally required at all jobs, this candidate should have answered differently.

Q Your GPA wasn't very high. Can you please explain that?

A During my first two years of college, I was kind of immature and didn't work hard enough. I worked really hard my junior and senior years, but unfortunately those first two years really brought down my GPA. It was hard to recover from that.

This candidate acknowledges that she was responsible for her low GPA but also talks about how she worked hard to raise it.

Never Say: "Just bad luck, I guess."

Q What was your favorite thing about high school?

A My favorite thing about high school was working on the school newspaper. I was the managing editor during my senior year. I learned how to stick to deadlines and I helped our editors organize projects on which they were working.

The interviewee picked something that allowed him to show two of his skills—time management and organization. He knows that employers in his field value these skills.

Never Say: "I loved everything about high school." While the interviewer may appreciate the candidate's positive attitude, this answer doesn't tell her anything about him.

 **Question**

> **How should I explain poor grades?**
> With few exceptions, you earned your grades, whether they were good or bad, so you should always take full responsibility for them. Explain what happened without appearing to beat yourself up, e.g., don't say "I was such an idiot." If you can, discuss the measures you took to improve your GPA. You can also talk about what you could have done differently.

Q What did you like most about college?

A I really enjoyed playing on the volleyball team. During my freshman and sophomore years the team wasn't as strong as it could have been. We pulled together and worked very hard, and by my junior year we were ranked number two in our division. By my senior year we were in first place.

This candidate's mention of his participation on an athletic team draws attention to his ability to work on a team. From his research, he learned that this company's employees often work on teams, so he decided this was a good opportunity to show off this attribute.

Never Say: "I loved my classes." While that is admirable, this candidate doesn't say why this is so. If his classes were truly his favorite part of college, he needs to explain how his own actions contributed to his feeling that way.

Q Why did you choose to go away to college rather than going to a school closer to your home?

A I wanted to be responsible for myself, and I knew that wouldn't happen at home. By living in the dorms, I had no choice but to manage my own time, budget my money, and set my own limits.

This candidate saw going away to college as a learning experience, both in and out of the classroom, and presents it that way to the interviewer.

Never Say: "My parents didn't like the boy I was dating, so they sent me away to school." Have you ever heard of giving too much information?

Q Why didn't you go to college?

A I didn't know what I wanted to do at the time and I didn't want to waste my parents' money. I thought I would gain more from working than I would from school. Now that I have work experience and I know I want to stay in this field, I plan to get my degree. The city university has a program that accommodates working adults.

The interviewee's decision to postpone college, as he explains it, was a clearly thought-out one. While he indicates his intention to continue his education, he is also quick to point out that it won't affect his work schedule.

Never Say: "I don't know. I didn't really give it much thought." Not giving a lot of thought to such an important decision doesn't say much about this applicant, or maybe it says too much.

Q Why didn't you finish college?

A I left school because of financial reasons. My parents couldn't afford my tuition, so I decided to work for a few years. The experience was actually a great one for me. I learned a lot from it. I'm planning to take some classes next semester. I just heard about a great program that offers classes online. I even checked the program out with the state education department and it's legitimate.

Dropping out of school for financial reasons is certainly legitimate. This candidate speaks positively of her work experience, claiming she gained something from it. She goes on to explain how her plan to take some classes won't affect her work schedule, something the employer would probably appreciate.

Never Say: "I didn't really like school that much." This interviewee gives the impression that she doesn't make well-informed decisions.

Chapter 7

Discussing Your Work History

WHILE EXPERIENCE ISN'T everything, it does count for a lot when a prospective employer must decide between you and other qualified candidates. What you have done in your past jobs is significant and an interviewer will spend a lot of time learning about your work history so he can discover how it will affect your future performance. That is why it is so important that you take great care to present your past well.

How to Present Your Past

What does it mean to present your past well? After years of spending many of your waking hours working, here's a chance to let your past jobs work for you. Answering questions about your work history gives you the opportunity to highlight things you want to call to a prospective employer's attention. At the same time, you want to downplay things on which you would rather not have her focus. You want to tell your side of the story in your own words and in greater depth than you could ever do on a resume.

When prospective employers ask questions about your work history, they want to know more than where you worked, how long you worked there, and what your job duties were. They can learn that from your resume. They would love to hear about the skills you gained at each of your previous jobs, but that information is probably on your resume as well. Now it's time to get beyond the resume and learn more about you than they ever could from a one- or two-page document. Employers want to know not only what skills you picked up on your prior jobs, but how you used those skills. They want to know what you liked about each job, and what you didn't like. They want to find out if you got along with your boss. Employers want to know why you left each of your jobs, or why you stayed. They want to know what motivates you. They want to know how your career has progressed and how you expect it to progress in the future. Most importantly, employers want to know what you can bring to them as an employee.

Essential

As you prepare to answer questions about your work history, use your resume to guide you. Look at each job and try to recall specific details about every one. Write down those facts and commit them to memory. Preparing in advance can help save you from awkward moments of silence as you try to answer a prospective employer's questions.

When you give answers to questions about your work history, make every one count. Each response should tell the interviewer how your experience qualifies you for this particular job. You should give specific examples drawn from your experiences. When an interviewer asks if you've ever performed a particular activity on a past job she generally expects more than a yes or no answer. As with every type of question so far, you must give detailed answers.

Questions and Answers

Q What was your first job?

A My very first job was in a deli. I worked there every summer from ninth grade until I graduated from college. At first I was hired to do odd jobs, but once I was old enough, I worked behind the counter serving customers. I was the youngest employee there, but my boss always said I was the hardest-working one.

By discussing his longevity on this job, as well as his former boss's favorable opinion of him, this candidate lets the interviewer know he was a valued employee. He doesn't dwell on the fact that the job was not in his current career field.

Never Say: "It was just in a deli." This candidate needs to give more details about his job and use it to show off his attributes.

Q Out of the jobs you've had, which was your favorite?

A My favorite job was teaching at the Wee Ones Preschool. I like my current job at Parkside Elementary, but I realize now that I prefer to work with preschoolers. That's why I want to work here.

This candidate has chosen to discuss a job that is related to the one for which she is being interviewed.

Never Say: "I loved working at Sam's Steakhouse in college. The other waitresses and I had so much fun together." Not only does this candidate choose a job unrelated to her chosen field, she doesn't sound very serious about working at all.

Q Tell me about your current job.

A I am a junior architect at James, Jones, and Johnson. I work in the commercial building division. As part of a team of five architects, I help design shopping centers and office complexes.

The interviewee describes his current job as he is asked to do. He discusses his work as part of a team because he knows that this prospective employer also utilizes a team structure.

Never Say: "I work at James, Jones, and Johnson. It's right there on my resume." The interviewer wants the candidate to give a detailed description of his current job. Since it is probable that he has already read the resume, it does the candidate no good to simply reiterate what is there.

Q Tell me about a typical day at work.

A Every day is different. The one constant is that I spend from two to three hours working at the reference desk each day, assisting patrons. That leaves either four or five hours to tend to what I refer to as "behind the scenes" work. I'm in charge of library publicity, so I might have to write and send out press releases or update our mailing list. If it's the middle of the month, I'll be working on the monthly newsletter. When I'm not working on publicity, I'm selecting books to order or weeding outdated material from our collection.

The candidate takes this opportunity to discuss her many responsibilities.

Never Say: "Every day is different. I do so many things, it's hard to say what a typical day is." This person indicates she's busy, but she needs to talk about what her responsibilities are.

Q What do you like about your job?

A I like it when I can successfully resolve a customer's problem. If the customer walks away satisfied, I'm happy.

By giving this answer, the candidate shows that keeping customers happy motivates him. This is surely something this employer will see as a positive trait, since happy customers are repeat customers.

Never Say: "My boss is nice." While speaking well of your boss is good, this candidate should have chosen something about his job that gives him satisfaction.

Essential

When you are asked to discuss something you like about your job, choose something that is related to your work. Talk about job duties, specifically ones that are related to those you will have if you are hired by the company with which you are interviewing. Try to demonstrate how you have benefited your employer by performing these tasks well.

Q What kinds of jobs did you have during college?

A I had a variety of jobs while I was going to college, and since I was paying my own way I sometimes had more than one job. I worked as a waiter, a door-to-door salesman, and a data entry clerk. I learned a lot about interacting tactfully with different people, and I also developed my office and computer skills.

In addition to demonstrating how industrious she is (working her way through school), this candidate shows how she developed skills in different areas through her experience.

Never Say: "I just had some menial jobs." No matter how menial she thought those jobs were, she should have taken the time to figure out what skills they helped her develop.

Q Describe your favorite boss.

A That would have to be my boss at Triangle Optical. Paul was the most demanding boss I've ever had. He expected so much from our department. What set him apart from other supervisors was that he worked tirelessly alongside us and he was just as demanding of himself. He always gave everyone the credit they deserved.

This applicant values having a demanding boss. In addition, by telling her prospective employer what traits she valued in a former boss, this applicant is letting him know what she will be like as a supervisor if she is hired for this job.

Never Say: "I like a boss who is flexible and fair." While the candidate doesn't reveal anything negative by giving this answer, she should be more specific.

Q Describe your least favorite boss.

A I'd rather not mention names since this industry is so small. I had a boss who never planned anything in advance. We were always racing to meet deadlines, running out of supplies, or finding ourselves short staffed because she couldn't say no to anyone who asked for a day off.

While it's generally best not to say something negative about a former employer, the interviewee must answer the question. In saying he won't reveal the name of his least favorite boss, he demonstrates tact and discretion. He is also somewhat restrained in his criticism. All this candidate says is that he prefers someone who is more structured. Rejecting his former boss's management style implies that this is not what he'd be like as a manager.

Never Say: "Her name was Josephine Josephson and she was my boss at BRK Audio. She was too demanding." This applicant doesn't hesitate to reveal his boss's name and doesn't give enough of a reason for choosing her as his worst boss. The interviewer may be left wondering why he considered this person too demanding.

Q You seem to be climbing the corporate ladder in your current job. Why leave now?

A I'm choosing to leave now because my goals have changed. I feel I can better use my public relations skills at a nonprofit organization such as this one.

This applicant is making a change to another industry, but shows how she can still utilize her skills to meet her new goals.

Never Say: "My bosses are crazy. I can't stay there anymore." Remember that making negative comments about any employer is a bad idea.

Q I see three jobs listed on your resume. Can you tell me what you learned from each of them?

A I learned a lot on each of my jobs, so it's hard to pick one thing from each, but I'll try. When I worked in customer support at CSV, I learned how to help our software users troubleshoot problems. When I worked as a software trainer at Circle Tech, I learned that I needed to find a common ground when teaching a large group of people, because not everyone has the same level of skills. I learned to manage employees at my job as assistant to the head of training at APCO.

Knowing about the job that he's applying for helped the applicant answer this question. He has picked one skill from each of his previous jobs that will be required for the position with this employer.

Never Say: "I learned to be at work on time from my first job. Then from my second job, I learned to keep my mouth shut." While it's good that the applicant has learned these things, they don't demonstrate why he will be a valuable employee.

Q Do you find your job rewarding?

A I found my job very rewarding for a long time, but lately it hasn't been as rewarding. While I love my new responsibilities, I miss working with clients. That is what attracted me to this position—the combination of supervisory responsibilities and client contact.

It's okay for the interviewee to say she doesn't find her current job rewarding. She explains why she feels this way without placing blame anywhere. With this answer, she also shows she knows about the position for which she's interviewing and explains why she is better suited for it.

Never Say: "No, I don't. When the new manager came in he took away everything I liked about my job." This candidate sounds angry.

Q What about your current job isn't very rewarding?

A I think every job has something about it that isn't rewarding. There is a lot of paperwork and I don't find that particularly rewarding, but I know it needs to be done.

This candidate understands the reality of work. Some job duties are rewarding, while others are not. She chose something that many people don't find particularly rewarding—paperwork.

Never Say: "Everything about it is rewarding." The interviewer, who knows every job has things about it that are not rewarding, will question this applicant's sincerity. Furthermore, he will wonder why the applicant is leaving her current job if she finds everything about it rewarding.

Q How have your other jobs prepared you for the one at this company?

A I've worked on the retail end of the office supplies industry for the past ten years. I know what customers want and what the retail outlets want. I know the industry and I know the products. That is what qualifies me to be a sales rep for Roxy Staple Company.

This candidate shows confidence in her abilities as a salesperson and in her knowledge of the industry of which the prospective employer is a part.

Never Say: "I learned a lot on my previous jobs. My skills qualify me for a job with your company." By giving such a brief answer, the interviewer will have to follow up with the question, "Which skills would those be?"

Q Your last job was very different than the ones you had before it and very different than this one. Why did you take that job?

A I was thinking of going back to school to be a veterinarian. I mentioned this to my neighbor, a vet, and he offered me a job in his office. I love animals, but before I made the commitment to go to veterinary school, I wanted to make sure I'd be happy working with them and especially dealing with sick ones. It turned out that wasn't right for me after all.

This candidate has a good explanation for why she took a job that deviated from her career path. In providing it, she also shows off her decision-making skills—she didn't jump into a new career without careful consideration.

Never Say: "The job was available and they wanted to hire me." This candidate had no particular reason for taking a job outside her field, leading the potential employer to question her goals.

Q How do you feel about the way your department was managed on your last job?

A I think it was managed effectively.

This isn't a glowing review, but the candidate didn't say anything negative, either. Even if he thinks his manager was a bumbling fool, he avoids saying so. Badmouthing his boss would make the applicant look bad.

Never Say: "The manager was awful." Making a negative statement like this one is generally not a good idea, but if he has to do it, he should give more of an explanation that would back up his claims.

Q You've never worked in widget manufacturing before. How have your jobs in the publishing industry prepared you for this?

A Taking a product, whether it's a widget or a book, from its inception to the hands of the consumer takes a lot of planning. You have to put together a budget and set deadlines. You need to make sure your current staff can handle the work and hire consultants if necessary. You may even have to handle crises along the way, should problems arise. I dealt with such things on a daily basis while working in publishing, and I would be able to use the same planning and management skills to help your company.

By focusing on her job responsibilities and talking about them in general terms, this candidate is able to show how she can transfer her skills from one industry to another.

Never Say: "I had to work long hours in publishing and I know people in your industry work long hours, too." This doesn't tell the interviewer much about the candidate or what skills she has.

Q How would your current supervisor describe you?

A Mr. Roberts respects me. He would describe me as a diligent worker who takes great care to do an excellent job on every project he assigns to me. I complete all work on time. He appreciates the fact that I am very friendly and usually asks me to be our department's "welcome wagon" when a new employee starts.

A little bit of bragging on a job interview is a good thing. This applicant knows that to answer with anything less than this amount of confidence might lead the interviewer to think she's unsure of himself.

Never Say: "I've worked there for three years and he's never complained." Saying your boss never complained about you doesn't exactly shout "great employee!"

Q What decisions have you had to make on your current job?

A When I planned career workshops for students, I had to decide what topics to feature, when to hold the workshops, and who would speak at them. I had to decide what software to purchase for our public computers within the constraints of our budget. I also made decisions about hiring and firing student aides.

By giving specific examples, this candidate highlights his skills in planning events, making purchasing decisions, working within a budget, and making personnel decisions.

Never Say: "I didn't really get to make too many decisions." This applicant should realize the interviewer is asking this question because decision-making is required on this job. He should take a moment to think of one or two decisions he has made. Even if they don't seem significant, it is better than not giving an answer.

Q What were the reasons you went to work for your two prior employers?

A I went to work for Pear Computers right out of college. They had an excellent one-year training program, and I knew I would learn a lot there. After I completed the training program, I stayed there for three years. I went to work for my next employer, Bell Technology, because they offered me a position with greater responsibilities than Pear Computers could.

This candidate takes advantage of the opportunity to mention her participation in a training program where she was able to enhance what she learned in school. When she says she stayed at the company for a while after taking part in the training program, she demonstrates her loyalty—she didn't just take the training and run. Her next job was clearly a step up from her first one, which shows how her career has progressed so far.

Never Say: "Each of my last two employers offered a good salary and benefits." This applicant should better demonstrate how she makes decisions. More thought should go into choosing to go to work for someone.

Q Why did you leave your last job?

A I left my last job because I knew the industry was facing an uncertain future. I researched this industry, saw the growth potential, and knew I could make a significant contribution.

This job candidate shows that he knows how to plan for the future. He doesn't make decisions without doing his homework first.

Never Say: "I was bored." Without giving further explanation, this isn't a good enough reason to leave your job.

Q You've been at your job for several years. What makes you want to leave?

A I've completed what I set out to do. When I first started working there, the company was just getting started. They needed someone who had the skills to help them grow. They are very successful now and I feel like I've completed my mission. I know I could better use my skills in a growing company such as yours.

Not only does this applicant show off her accomplishments at her current job, she tells her potential employer what she can do for his company.

Never Say: "I want to make more money." This may really be this candidate's reason for leaving her job, but it isn't a good enough one to give to a prospective employer.

Q How is your present job different from the ones you had before it?

A As a senior accounting clerk, I supervise three payroll clerks and a bookkeeper. This is the first time I've had to supervise people.

By discussing her increased responsibilities, this applicant shows how she has moved up in her career.

Never Say: "I have to use a computer now and I also have to work late." Neither of these things illustrates the candidate's growth.

Q What duties of your last job did you find difficult?

A I found it difficult to fire people. Even though I always put a lot of thought into deciding whether or not to terminate someone, I knew I was affecting someone's livelihood.

No one could fault someone for disliking this unpleasant duty.

Never Say: "Dealing with my boss every day." Oops.

Q Describe how your career progressed over the last five years. Was it aligned with the goals you set for yourself?

A When I graduated from the community college, I knew I wanted to be a store manager. I also knew I would have to work my way up, so I took a job as a sales associate at Dress Corral. After two years, and a lot of hard work, I was promoted to assistant department manager. After being in that job for a year, P. J. Coopers hired me to be manager of the ladies' accessories department. I've been there for the last two years. With my experience, I'm ready for the next step—store manager.

This job candidate shows exactly how his career has progressed and how he is now ready for a job with this employer.

Never Say: "I really didn't set any goals. I took the sales associate job because it was the only place that wanted someone with my skills. It's been nice to be able to move up." It's okay if this candidate didn't have a plan to start with, but he should have made one along the way. It seems he's let others set goals for him. If he doesn't have a plan, this prospective employer can't predict what he'll do next.

Q How would those who worked under you describe you as a supervisor?

A My staff at AQA Associates knew I was someone who worked hard and expected the same of them. They also felt I was fair, never asking them to do something I wasn't willing to do myself. My office door was always open and they felt they could come to me to discuss any problem they might have.

This applicant describes the qualities of a good supervisor. Not only does she tell the interviewer how her staff felt about her, she tells him why they felt that way. Notice how sure she is of her answer, never saying, "I think they felt this way." She knows exactly how she is regarded as a supervisor.

Never Say: "I think they thought I did a good job." The applicant doesn't provide enough information.

Q This job carries with it much more responsibility than you've had before. Are you ready?

A I am definitely ready. I've been working as assistant registrar for five years. I have learned a lot at Burberry College. I've worked very closely with my boss and I know what his job entails. He is also confident in my ability to move on.

This candidate restates her experience and shares with the interviewer the vote of confidence her boss gave her.

Never Say: "Sure. Why not? I've paid my dues."

Q Have you had to do any traveling for work?

A I've had to do some traveling for my job. I went to Asia several times. I enjoy traveling and hope to do more of it on this job. I find it helpful to have face-to-face meetings with clients periodically rather than doing everything through conference calls.

This applicant knows that his potential employer requires extensive traveling. Although he hasn't done a lot of it, he makes sure to point out that it's something he wants to do more.

Never Say: "They had me traveling all over the place." This candidate doesn't sound very enthusiastic.

Q What do you think this job offers that your last job did not?

A This job offers me the opportunity to use my research skills. I have mostly administrative duties on my current job, with some research duties. I look forward to a job that is primarily research oriented with some administrative duties.

This applicant has both administrative and research skills, as she points out to the interviewer. She wants to use them in a different way than she does on her current job. She knows, based on what she has learned about this position, that research is a big part of the job.

Never Say: "This job offers me the opportunity to do research. I've always wanted to do that." There's nothing to indicate that this person has any research skills. If there are many candidates from which to choose, the employer may not be willing to hire someone who still requires training.

Q What kind of person do you find it difficult to work with? What kind of person do you find it easy to work with?

A I find it difficult to work with someone who does sloppy work, takes credit when he hasn't earned it, or tries to get away with doing as little as possible. I find it easy to work with someone who is ambitious, takes the time to do the best job possible, and does more than is asked of her.

"That's not me" is what the interviewee is really saying when he reveals which traits he doesn't like in a coworker. Ambitious, does the best job possible—"now, that's me," the job candidate is saying.

Never Say: "I don't like working with someone who isn't friendly. I much prefer someone who wants to hang out after work." The traits this candidate brings up have little to do with work.

Q How do you think your boss will react when you tell her you're leaving?

A I've already discussed it with her, so she won't be surprised. She doesn't want to lose me, but she knows I'm ready for more responsibility, and she can't offer that to me. The only job with more responsibility than I currently have is hers.

By giving this answer the job candidate clearly demonstrates that he has a good relationship with his boss.

Never Say: "I think she's going to be very upset. I don't know how she's going to replace me." While it's appropriate to be very confident on a job interview, this candidate is being very unrealistic if he thinks he's irreplaceable.

Q What was your salary when you started your current job and what is it now?

A I earned $40,000 per year when I started and now, after five years, I'm up to $50,000.

As long as this information is accurate, this is a good answer.

Never Say: "I'm not sure what I made when I started, but I'm making $50,000 per year now." The candidate should be ready to provide this information; if she truly doesn't know the answer, she can offer to provide it later.

Chapter 8

Your Interpersonal Skills

WOULDN'T IT BE nice if everyone got along with one another? Unfortunately, a world in which everyone gets along is only a dream. There will always be personality conflicts and differences of opinions, whether they are within families, on the playground, or at work. They cannot be avoided. What is important is how we deal with conflicts and differences of opinion when they occur. If handled well, they can lead to new ideas and growth.

An Employee Balancing Act

Each time an employer introduces a new member to his company or department, he disturbs a delicate balance. Depending on how well the new employee gets along with her new coworkers, this addition may completely tip the scales in one direction or another, or they may move only slightly.

Any change could cause a drop in productivity. An existing employee may find it difficult to concentrate on work when he is worried about what the new coworker meant when she gave him "that look" a few minutes ago. Serious drops in productivity occur when coworkers are too busy arguing to get any work done.

Chapter 3 discussed the personal questions you may be asked on an interview. Employers ask personal questions so they can learn about your personality or character traits. One reason they want to know about this is so they can determine whether you will fit in with the other company employees. These character traits are only a piece of the puzzle, however. A potential employee may have skills and experience that make her the most qualified candidate, but her character traits may differ greatly from those of other employees. This probably won't matter to the employer as long as the candidate knows how to make the most of those differences instead of getting sidetracked by them and causing productivity to suffer.

Essential

A potential employer will try to find out if you are someone who either causes conflicts or doesn't know how to resolve them when they occur. If you indicate that you have a tendency to have difficulties getting along with others, a red flag will go up and he will be less likely to hire you.

How Do You Resolve Conflicts?

When an employer is trying to find out how you interact with others, she may ask questions about hypothetical situations. For example, you may be asked how you would resolve a problem with a coworker. Alternatively, the interviewer may ask you to discuss times you actually did experience conflict with another individual. You should always present a balanced look at those situations. Everyone knows there are three sides to every story—your side, the other person's side, and the truth. Instead of taking sides, try to offer a look at the situation from everyone's point of view and talk about how you effectively dealt with the problem and solved it. Just as you should avoid placing all the blame on someone else, you should also avoid taking all the blame yourself.

An employer may be interested in knowing how you resolve serious conflicts before they escalate. Too often we hear about an angry employee losing control and doing something to physically harm his employer or coworkers. Your prospective employer will want to know you are a calm and reasonable person who doesn't let her anger get out of hand. If you are interviewing for a supervisory position, the interviewer will want to know whether you have the ability to defuse other people's anger.

 Fact

Workplace violence is an issue in modern American society. The U.S. Occupational Safety and Health Administration estimated that there were 2 million victims of workplace violence in 2002. OSHA has suggestions for making the workplace a safer place on its website, *www.osha.gov.*

Questions and Answers

Q Unfortunately every office has personality conflicts. What do you do when you work with someone you don't particularly like?

A While I know you don't have to be buddies with all your colleagues, workplaces are more productive if everyone gets along. I would try to resolve my differences with that person. If that wasn't possible, I'd find something about that person I could admire and respect and I'd focus on that instead of the things I didn't like.

This applicant shows he's proactive when he says he would try to work out his differences with his coworker but realistic when he says that if he can't, he will find something to respect about his coworker.

Never Say: "I get along with everyone, so this won't be a problem." Is this person too good to be true? Probably.

Essential

Being assertive and being aggressive aren't the same thing. Those who are assertive are self-assured, aren't afraid to express their opinions, and are adept at the art of gentle persuasion. People who are aggressive are more likely to force their opinion on others, which often causes problems in a work environment. Most employers value workers who are assertive but not aggressive.

Q Describe the relationship that should exist between a supervisor and a subordinate.

A The relationship between a supervisor and a subordinate should be professional, yet friendly. At one of my earlier jobs I had a supervisor who set a perfect example for what this relationship should be like. She always acted professionally but also seemed interested in her workers as people. For example, she made a point of asking us if we had a nice weekend and how things were going, but she never pried into our personal lives. She was friendly without trying to be our friend.

This interviewee not only correctly states what the relationship between a supervisor and subordinate should be, but he also talks about his role model for such a relationship.

Never Say: "Strictly professional." This applicant should elaborate on his answer.

Q What would you do if you disagreed with your boss?

A It would depend on the situation. If I disagreed with her about whether the office is warm or cold I might not say anything. However, if I disagreed with my boss about whether the new marketing campaign was going to work, I'd share my thoughts with her.

This applicant knows he has to choose his battles wisely. There's a difference between being disagreeable and disagreeing.

Never Say: "I would never tell my boss I disagreed with her." This applicant is too passive.

Q What do you expect someone you supervise to do if she disagrees with you?

A I would expect that person to let me know what she's thinking. It could influence my decision. If she doesn't share her thoughts with me, I won't have the opportunity to hear her take on things.

This job candidate respects his coworkers' opinions. He knows it wouldn't be wise to make decisions without taking their comments into consideration.

Never Say: "Disagreeing with your supervisor? Isn't that a little disrespectful?" This candidate's answer implies that he is more interested in his own image and power than in his company's success.

Q What would you do if your supervisor handed you an assignment but you didn't quite understand it?

A I would first make sure I didn't just need to take a closer look at the project to better understand it. Once I did that, I would ask questions if I needed to. I'd rather ask questions before I begin than have to correct mistakes later on.

This candidate tries to work independently when possible, but knows that clarification is sometimes necessary and is not afraid to ask for it.

Never Say: "I would try to figure it out on my own." This interviewee is trying to show that she is independent but her answer may send up red flags. The employer will wonder if this independence will cause the candidate to make mistakes.

Q What would you do if your boss asks you do something that is clearly not part of your job description?

A It would depend on what it was I was asked to do. I wouldn't expect to run personal errands for my boss, but if I were asked to do something to help the company that wasn't normally part of my job, I wouldn't have a problem with it.

With this answer, the applicant shows his flexibility. However, this extends only to situations where the request is appropriate. If the boss is looking for someone to run her personal errands and that is something the candidate refuses to do, it's better to set things straight right from the start.

Never Say: "I would do anything I was asked to do." While flexibility is important, no one should be a pushover.

Q How did you get along with your last supervisor?

A We had a great relationship. I really respected him and I know he respected me, too. My supervisor knew he could trust me with any project, so he always assigned me those that were very challenging.

This candidate describes her relationship with her boss on a professional level, yet manages to say something very positive about herself.

Never Say: "We got along so well. We had lunch together all the time." It sounds like this interviewee is describing a buddy, not a supervisor.

Q How do you evaluate the work of others?

A Giving a critical opinion of someone's work is very tricky. Some people are more receptive than others, so I try to be careful while still getting my point across. I always make sure to talk about what someone has done right before mentioning what he has done wrong. I offer guidance to help my subordinates make the changes they need to, yet I give them room to make their own decisions.

This candidate shows that she knows how to handle a potentially sticky situation. She respects her subordinates and wants to maintain a good relationship with them. That, however, doesn't stop her from offering criticism when it is necessary.

Never Say: "I'm always straightforward. If someone doesn't want to be criticized, he should do a good job in the first place." A supervisor should know how to be diplomatic. This candidate shows that diplomacy isn't her strong suit.

Q What would you do if a member of your staff seemed upset about something but you didn't know what the problem was?

A I would ask if he wanted to talk about what's bothering him and make sure he knew I was available. If he didn't want to talk, I wouldn't push because it might be something personal. However, if it were work-related, I would hope he'd be able to be honest about it so we'd be able to solve the problem together.

This candidate demonstrates both sensitivity and professionalism with this answer. She is sensitive to the needs of her staff and indicates that she is approachable, especially when it comes to work-related issues.

Never Say: "I have to maintain a distance between myself and my staff. If there's something I need to know, my employee should come to me. If it's a personal problem, he can just leave it at home where it belongs." This candidate shows that she hasn't yet developed an understanding of what it means to be a good manager.

Alert

Employers want managers who can strike a balance between compassion and professionalism when dealing with their subordinates. They prefer managers who don't become so personally involved with their staff members that it clouds their judgment, but, at the same time, are approachable and understanding.

Q Have you ever had a boss you didn't like?

A Of course I've worked for some bosses I've liked more than others, but I try to stay professional and always make an effort to get along with everyone.

"Never complain about a former boss" is the line that keeps running through this candidate's head. Rather than do that, he keeps his answer as positive as possible.

Never Say: "Have I ever! Let me tell you about my last boss." This candidate seems eager to talk about his employer behind her back. Is that the kind of person the interviewer wants around his office?

Q What would you do if your company implemented a policy you disagreed with?

A Before taking any action I would need to evaluate the situation. I would have to determine whether I just needed time to get used to the new policy or if the policy had serious flaws that would affect the well-being of the company. If I determined that the latter was true, I would express my disapproval as soon as possible. It's difficult to be the one to make waves, but I would have to look out for the company. I wouldn't just criticize the new policy; I would suggest ways to make useful changes.

This interviewee demonstrates that she stops to think before taking action. However, if she determines she needs to take action, she does so in a constructive way. She looks out for her employer's welfare and puts the interests of the company first.

Never Say: "I don't like making waves. I'd probably just keep my mouth shut." This candidate's answer tells the interviewer she isn't proactive.

Q What would you do if you received what you felt was an unfair evaluation?

A I would wait a little while before I approached my supervisor—probably until the next morning. I wouldn't want to talk to my supervisor while I was angry because I might say the wrong thing. I would write down point-by-point why I thought the evaluation was inaccurate. Then I would present my thoughts to my supervisor calmly.

This candidate shows that he does not act on emotion. He takes the time to evaluate a situation before making a move. After doing that he makes an effort to calmly present his case.

Never Say: "I'd march right into her office and tell her how wrong she is." The last thing an employer wants is an employee who acts on his emotions. A job candidate should come across as someone who thinks carefully before he acts or speaks.

Q What would you do if someone you supervised came to you because he felt your evaluation of him was unfair?

A I would ask him to explain to me why he thought the evaluation was unfair. If he had a valid argument to back up his claim, I would reconsider the evaluation. If not, I would sit down with him to discuss what improvements could be made so that his next evaluation would be better.

This interviewee illustrates how she takes the time to listen to her subordinates. She shows she is willing to make changes to the evaluation if she realizes she needs to, but if not, will help the employee improve.

Never Say: "I'm really careful when I write evaluations, so they are always accurate." This job candidate doesn't realize that everyone makes mistakes, even those who are really careful.

Q Describe the ideal coworker.

A The ideal coworker is one who respects those around him. He doesn't engage in behavior that would be offensive to others. He offers constructive criticism and accepts it as well. He contributes to the department and company and doesn't try to compete with his coworkers. He shares responsibility for victories as well as defeats.

This applicant lists a number of desirable qualities and shows that he understands what makes a good employee. Hopefully this candidate is also describing traits he possesses.

Never Say: "I prefer someone who keeps to himself. I really don't want to make friends at work." If this is what this candidate believes, he will have trouble being part of a congenial environment.

Q Describe the ideal manager.

A The ideal manager expects a lot of her employees. She respects them. She knows their individual abilities and makes sure they utilize them to the fullest. She continually challenges them to do more and recognizes their accomplishments.

This answer can mean one of two things. The candidate may be describing her own abilities as a manager. In that case, this is a manager who will retain a productive staff. Alternatively, she could be describing the type of manager she'd like to work under. If that is the case, an employee who likes to work under a supervisor who expects a lot is someone who is willing to live up to those expectations.

Never Say: "The ideal manager is one who doesn't interfere too much with her employees. I like someone who just lets everyone do their jobs." If this candidate is describing herself as a manager, she shows that she lacks managerial skills. If she is describing a manager she'd like to work for, she has shown herself as a worker who, for some reason, doesn't want anyone to know what she is doing.

Q Describe the ideal employee.

A The ideal employee is one who always does more than he is asked to do. He is open to challenges and is always willing to learn more and take on more responsibilities. He is also receptive to constructive criticism.

Hopefully this candidate has described himself, and any employer would be happy to have an employee like this.

Never Say: "The ideal employee is one who does what is asked of him. He doesn't ask a lot of questions." This candidate, if describing himself, sounds weak.

Q What would you do if someone came to you to complain about his supervisor?

A First, I would ask him if he had talked to his supervisor yet. If not, I would ask him to do that first. I would make sure he knew how to approach the supervisor and offer him tips if he didn't. If he had already talked to his supervisor but hadn't gotten anywhere with her, I would have him tell me his side of the story. Next, I would talk to his supervisor to get her side of the story. After considering what both people had told me, I would decide how to resolve the problem.

This job candidate shows he knows how to follow protocol when he says he would ask the employee to speak to his supervisor first. He demonstrates that he won't take sides and must hear both sides of a story before deciding what to do.

Never Say: "I'd listen to what he had to say and then call his supervisor down to my office so I could deal with the problem immediately." This interviewee indicates that he wastes no time, but this is not the best way to deal with a serious problem.

⛯ Alert

Every work environment is different, and the interviewer wants to know if you will succeed in this one. Employers put a lot of effort into making sure they hire the most suitable candidates possible. The candidate must be able to carry out the necessary job duties, and she must fit in well with the other employees.

Q What would your current coworkers say about you?

A My coworkers would say I'm very committed to my job. I work hard to contribute to each project's success and I always share credit with everyone else who contributes to that success.

This interviewee portrays herself as someone who is a team player. She sticks to talking about work-related matters.

Never Say: "They would say they like me." That's nice, but the applicant should try to think up something a little more concrete to show why she is a good employee.

Q What would you do about a long-term employee whose work has been slipping lately?

A I would talk to my employee to find out what was going on. Obviously if this person always did a good job, something must have happened to change that. As a supervisor, it is my job to find out what that is and help the employee fix the problem; it is also preferable to firing someone. It is generally more cost effective to retain a worker who already knows the job than to train someone new. It also is better for the morale of that person's coworkers, who don't want to see a coworker lose his job.

This answer shows that the candidate has good managerial skills. While dismissing an unproductive employee may seem like a quick and easy solution in the short term, it can have a detrimental effect on the company in the end.

Never Say: "Whoever doesn't pull his weight has to go. I would just fire the employee." This candidate may know how to solve a problem quickly, but she doesn't account for the repercussions.

Q What would you do if an important client asked you out on a date?

A I would politely decline, explaining that I make a point of never mixing business with pleasure. I would then thank him and end the conversation as quickly as possible.

Good answer. This candidate won't compromise her integrity.

Never Say: "How important is this client?"

Q Have you ever had to persuade someone to accept your point of view? How did you do it and were you successful?

A I have had to do that several times. A few months ago, for example, we were in the process of planning a new publication. We were deciding whether to hire a permanent employee or a freelancer to edit it. My manager felt we should go with a permanent employee. After analyzing the options, I felt strongly that hiring a freelancer would work best. I presented him with my reasons for wanting to hire a freelancer, including a cost analysis. I convinced my manager to try it my way, and so far it has worked out very well.

This interviewee gives an example that explains how she gathered information to help her make a decision and then presented the information to her manager to persuade him that this was the best choice.

Never Say: "I've had to do that several times. I can always get people to come around to my point of view." It is unclear how this candidate persuades others to come around to her point of view. Is she assertive or aggressive?

Q How do you handle an angry employee?

A Way too often you hear about an employee whose anger turns to violence. As a supervisor it would be my job to recognize potentially volatile situations. Once I recognized a problem, I would help the employee remove herself from the situation long enough to cool down. I would tell her where she could go for help.

This applicant knows anger can be serious and what to do before it escalates.

Never Say: "I'd fire her." This applicant shows that he knows how to further escalate a potentially violent situation.

Q What do you do when you have a very unhappy customer?

A My first step is to let the customer know I will listen to what she has to say. If the company has a strict policy regarding customer complaints, I will follow it. However, if I must use my own judgment, I would strike a balance between keeping the customer happy and not costing my employer too much. If I see that the customer's complaint is legitimate, I will do what it takes to remedy the situation.

This applicant plays by the rules. He knows a satisfied customer will return, but he also realizes that a company is always concerned about its bottom line.

Never Say: "The customer is always right. I will just give a customer what they want." If every customer is right, it will cost the company a lot of money.

⊱Ε⊰ Alert

Employers want to know that those they hire won't drive customers away. They want employees who know how to keep customers satisfied but will be attentive to the company's bottom line and not just hand out free stuff left and right.

Q A customer is extremely angry because, according to store policy, you can't accept an item she wants to return. How do you handle it?

A Sometimes you hear about these situations getting out of hand. If it looks like a situation may turn violent, I will do what is necessary to rectify it. If it costs the company a little money, well, the company's bottom line is important, but not as important as people's lives.

This job candidate shows he is practical. He has his priorities in order—lives before money.

Never Say: "Don't you worry. A customer's anger doesn't scare me. I'll always defend the company's policies." This candidate may be loyal, but his judgment is faulty.

Q As a supervisor, what do you do when employees working under you don't get along?

A I actually encountered this situation a few months ago. There were two employees in my department who were both very nice people, but they got off on the wrong foot when one of them transferred into the department. I called a meeting with them and asked them to try to resolve their differences for the good of the department. I can't actually say they like each other now, but there is a level of respect between them.

Nothing is better than a real-life experience. This job candidate was lucky enough to have one she could draw upon. She solved this problem in a very logical way and was very honest about the outcome.

Never Say: "It's really none of my business if my employees don't get along." Wrong answer. The interviewer has asked this question for a reason—a supervisor should be very concerned if two of her employees don't get along. She must deal with it.

Q If you were unhappy with your job, how would you discuss this with your boss?

A I've always had good relationships with everyone I've worked for, so I think it would be to everyone's benefit for me to be direct with my boss. First, I would make a list of the things I'm unhappy with, as well as suggestions for improving each situation. I would then ask for a meeting with my boss to go over the list point by point, being careful not to place any blame.

This interviewee smartly points out that he maintains a good relationship with his boss that can withstand this type of discussion. He explains how he would be proactive in helping to find a solution for the problems he is dealing with at work.

Never Say: "I don't think I'd bother discussing it. I would just look for another job." This answer may indicate that this candidate makes rash decisions and may not be loyal to this job if he gets it.

Q How do you handle criticism?

A I think criticism can be a valuable tool. It forces me to take a look at my own work to see how I can improve on it.

This candidate shows that she doesn't get all bent out of shape if someone has an unkind word for her.

Never Say: "If someone can't say something nice, maybe they shouldn't say anything at all."

Alert

Show that you can resolve problems on your own before you bring someone else into it. A candidate who indicates that she will go running to her supervisor to report difficulties with a coworker will be viewed by the interviewer as too high maintenance.

Q Suppose one of the people you supervise complains that his officemate is slacking off at work. How would you handle it?

A This happened to me at my last job. I already knew that the supposed slacker actually had higher productivity than the employee who complained. It's important to take such a complaint with a grain of salt. If this happened again I would politely tell the employee that I would handle the situation if necessary. Then I would keep an eye on the complainer, who apparently has too much time on her hands.

This manager portrays himself as someone who is very observant and is aware of what his staff is doing. He also handles the situation well by politely putting his employee in her place.

Never Say: "I would tell her to mind her own business." An effective supervisor needs to have a little more tact than that.

Q What would you do with an employee who seems to do her work very slowly? She gets her work done on time, but it's always very close to the deadline.

A Some people work more slowly than others. If her work is accurate and it's being completed before the deadline, I don't think there's anything to worry about.

The interviewee is very practical. He knows that everyone has different work styles and working quickly doesn't necessarily mean better performance.

Never Say: "I'd ask her to speed up and start asking for progress reports." This candidate sounds like someone who will cause unnecessary tension among the people he supervises.

Q The person in the next cubicle spends endless hours on the phone talking to his girlfriend. Not only is he not getting his work done but his chatter is keeping you from doing yours. What do you do?

A I would talk to him before I did anything else. He may not realize how loud his phone conversations are. I would politely let him know that I can hear what he's saying and hopefully that would be enough to get him to lower his volume. I might also consider getting a noise machine—something that plays soothing sounds—to block out his voice. If nothing else helped, I would try to move to another cubicle.

This job candidate shows that she's determined to solve problems on her own before involving her supervisor.

Never Say: "I would tell my supervisor. Who does this guy think he is, talking on the phone instead of working?" The prospective employer will see this interviewee as someone who will make waves. He has better things to do than worry about helping his employees solve petty disputes.

Chapter 9

Did You Do Your Homework?

RESEARCHING A PROSPECTIVE employer is one of the most important things you can do to prepare for a job interview. Chapter 1 advised you to keep up with the latest news about a company and find out about its line of business, financial condition, customers and clients, and the industry in which it operates. Arriving at the interview armed with this information shows the prospective employer how serious you are about the interview and about the job.

Proving Your Knowledge

During the course of a job interview, the person conducting it will ask you to discuss what you know about her company and the particular job for which she is hiring. Obviously, the interviewer is not asking you for this information because she wants or needs it herself. She wants to know you made an effort to do the research needed to get this information.

A job candidate who walks into an interview armed with knowledge about the employer demonstrates several things to the interviewer. He demonstrates that he isn't just looking for a job with *any* employer. He wants to work for this particular company because of what he knows about it. He also shows that he was ambitious enough to do the necessary research to learn what he could about the employer.

The interviewer may ask you direct questions regarding what you know about the company. If you haven't done your research, you won't be able to answer these questions. She will ask you about the company's services and its products. She may also ask you to talk about the industry of which the company is a part.

Essential

To find basic information about a prospective employer, start by looking at the company's website. You can learn about a company's product line and key personnel. Public companies often make their annual reports available on their websites. Some also provide a list of clients.

The interviewer may also ask you questions that aren't as straightforward. You may not even realize at first that she is testing your knowledge about the company. For example, the interviewer may ask you what you can contribute to the company and what changes you would make if you were hired. She may ask you why you want to work for the company and how this opportunity fits into your career plans. Base your answers to these questions on the information you gathered through your research.

Highlight Skills That Fit the Company

Throughout a job interview you will be asked many questions about your skills, work history, and accomplishments. The interviewer will ask you these questions because he wants to find out what you can bring to his company. The more you know about this employer, the better you can demonstrate that you have the particular attributes he values. Use what you have learned through your research to frame your answers. For example, if you learned that the company is in the process of expanding its web presence, talk about your skills, work history, and accomplishments in that area. Your goal is to not merely talk about your attributes in general terms. You will instead discuss them as they relate to this job in particular.

 Fact

> In order to become knowledgeable about a particular industry, you must learn as much as you can about it. The United States Bureau of Labor Statistics publishes industry information online. Industry at a Glance (*www.bls.gov/iag/iaghome.htm*), for example, provides information on more than 100 industries.

Questions and Answers

Q Now that you've told me about yourself, can you tell me what you know about us?

A Costello Laboratories is a pharmaceutical company with annual sales of over $15 billion. The company recently introduced a new medication to treat bipolar disorder, and I read that it is working on a new cardiac medication.

This answer shows that this candidate has done her homework. She knows what the company does and has even kept up with the latest news.

Never Say: "I haven't been able to find out anything about it." Unless you've been called for an interview an hour before it is to take place, there is no excuse for not doing your homework.

Q What do you think it takes to be successful here?

A I understand that Q & H Corporation introduced five new products to the market in the last year alone. In order to be a successful employee of such an innovative company, one would have to be very creative. In a competitive industry such as soaps and toiletries you need employees who can keep up with what consumers want.

This person has obviously done his homework. He not only knows about the company, but he seems to know about the industry as well.

Never Say: "In order to be successful, employees must work hard and do a good job." This can be said of employees of any company. If this candidate had done his homework, he would know more about this particular company.

Q Based on what you know about this company, how will you contribute to it?

A I see that most of your company's clients are in the food industry. Since I spent ten years working for AMJ Bean Company, I am very familiar with that industry. I know my experience in the industry is something your clients will appreciate.

This candidate has researched her prospective employer and knows that her experience in the food industry will help her should she be hired. She is able to make a point of mentioning that on the job interview.

Never Say: "I have great organizational skills and I can manage my time well." While most employers value these skills, the candidate does not explain why they will benefit this particular company.

Q There are a lot of companies that can use someone with your skills. Why do you want to work at this company?

A Home Warehouse has been more successful than any other company in the hardware industry. The company has seen steady profit growth over many years and it appears it will continue to do so. However, critics of the company are quick to point out that customer service is seriously lacking. As the director of customer service I will implement new procedures that will turn that negative image around.

This answer shows the interviewee's knowledge of the company, including its weaknesses. He already has a plan in mind to fix that weakness, as he shares with the interviewer.

Never Say: "I heard you pay really well." This candidate shows that he doesn't really know a lot about the company and how he will fit in as an employee.

Q What do you know about this industry?

A The retail industry is tremendous. It is the second largest industry in the United States, in terms of the numbers of both establishments and employees. There has been a decline in sales over recent years, but industry analysts think that will turn around when the economy improves.

This job candidate has done enough research to be able to intelligently discuss what she knows about the industry.

Never Say: "I don't know a lot about the retail industry. I've only worked in the financial industry, so this is all new to me." Knowledge about an industry does not have to come from experience. There are many resources this interviewee could have accessed to gather information.

Q Why do you want to work in this industry?

A I'm ready for a new challenge, and since more commercial banks have begun to offer investment services over the last few years, I know I can use the skills I learned as an investment banker to work in the commercial banking industry.

By giving this answer, the interviewee is able to demonstrate that he knows about this industry and what he can bring to it.

Never Say: "The hours are much better than they are in the investment banking industry." This answer doesn't show that the interviewee knows more about the industry than the number of hours one must work, and it certainly doesn't show what he can bring to it.

Q How much do you know about our company's recent growth?

A I know that XYZ Brands is a multinational company. I was particularly intrigued by your acquisition of ABC Corporation last March. It seems like it's going to open up a whole new market for this company.

Not only does the interviewee show that she took the time to learn about the company, she also shows she's kept up with the latest news about it. Notice that the interviewee said "it's going to open up a whole new market for this company" not "your company," so as not to create distance between herself and the employer.

Never Say: "I see your commercials on TV all the time, so you must be a pretty big company."

Q What interests you about our products and services?

A Turning Corporation provides products and services that help so many people. Just the other day I was reading about the new motorized scooter Turning developed. Those in health care and advocates for the disabled are very excited about it, according to everything I've read.

This candidate has obviously made a point of learning about his prospective employer, including keeping up with news about the latest products.

Never Say: "I don't know much about your products, but by the looks of your offices, they must sell really well."

Q Is there anything you've heard about our company that you don't like?

A It's really nothing specific to your company. I know the industry is a little shaky now, so of course I have some concerns about that. Based on what I've been reading, though, it looks like things are improving some.

This candidate shows that she did her homework, yet avoids bringing up anything that may cause awkward feelings. However, if there was something splashed across the front page of newspapers, the candidate would look ignorant if she didn't talk about it.

Never Say: "I heard you fire people who don't agree with you. Is that true?" That is something that might only be a rumor. Bringing it up during the interview could cause a lot of embarrassment.

Q Is there anything you find troubling about this industry?

A Actually, no. I've been reading a lot about this industry and everything I've seen so far is positive. This industry has made a great recovery after the decline about a decade ago. Since then it has been growing steadily and actually saw record growth last year.

Although he doesn't have anything negative to say, this candidate takes this opportunity to show that he did his homework.

Never Say: "No. It's nice to be in an industry like this, isn't it?" This interviewee may have done his homework, but he needs to elaborate on his answer to prove that.

Q Where do you think this company is going to be in five years?

A Based on what I've been reading it seems this company will be fully expanded into the international market by then. Parker Corporation opened offices in Japan and Switzerland last year, and I read that they are looking into opening Canadian offices next year.

This candidate is aware of what her prospective employer has in store for the future because she did her homework.

Never Say: "The future is always so fuzzy. Who can ever predict what is going to happen?" This interviewer didn't ask this candidate to look into a crystal ball. He wants her to make a prediction based on her current knowledge.

Q Do you know what your job duties will be if we hire you?

A As eligibility clerk, I know I will use my interviewing skills to help determine whether individuals are eligible to receive assistance from various government programs. I will interview people and then write reports that will be sent to the appropriate agencies.

Because she looked into it, this candidate knows what the general duties are for the job.

Never Say: "I didn't get a chance to look into that." The interviewer will wonder how this candidate can interview for a job she knows nothing about.

Q How does this job fit in with your career goals?

A As I mentioned earlier, my long-range goal is to be an elementary school principal. Reaching that is several years off, of course. I have a lot to learn about school administration. I've attended several workshops you've run and I am always impressed by your knowledge, and I know I can learn a lot from you. From what I've heard through the grapevine, you always place a lot of trust in everyone you hire and give employees a chance to grow. I know I can gain valuable knowledge and experience here at Oakwood, in addition to what I can contribute as an assistant principal.

This candidate demonstrates his knowledge about his prospective employer. He has personally learned from her in the past. He has also talked to other people who know her and how the school is run. Mentioning his aspiration to move beyond this job is a little bit risky, but since it will be quite a while before he can do that, he takes a chance.

Never Say: "It's an assistant principal job and clearly it's the next step I need to take in order to become a principal." In other words, this interviewee doesn't care where he gets his experience as long as he gets it.

Q If we hire you, what aspect of this job do you think you'll like best? What aspect of the job will you like least?

A I will enjoy working with clients one-on-one best, as I have in my previous position. The part I will like least is completing the massive quantity of paperwork that is required by all government agencies. However, I know it's a necessary part of this job and I've learned that if you keep up with it, it is much easier to deal with.

Demonstrating what she knows about the job, this candidate is able to discuss what she likes and doesn't like about it. She picks the major part of her job, working with clients, as the thing she likes best. When saying what she doesn't enjoy, she is upbeat and quick to point out that she knows it is necessary.

Never Say: "I love working with clients but I hate doing all the paperwork." It would have been better for this candidate not to be so vehement about her dislike of paperwork.

Q What would you like to accomplish here if we hire you?

A I read that this company is expanding into the children's clothing market. With my background in that area, I know I can help make that clothing line successful.

The interviewee bases his answer on what he has learned about this employer. He explains how his experience will help the company reach its goals.

Never Say: "I hope to move up to the executive suite." The candidate may have researched the layout of the office to determine that this suite exists, but that's not exactly the type of research that will impress a prospective employer.

Q Since all your experience has been in another industry, you must be a little concerned about making this change. What do you think working in this industry will be like?

A Everything in this industry seems to go at a very fast pace. I think the transition will be an easy one for me because in the magazine industry, I also worked at a fast pace. There were tight deadlines and sudden changes that needed to be dealt with on a moment's notice. From what I can tell, this industry involves the same things. I think I will be able to make a seamless transition to this industry.

This candidate's answer conveys that she has some knowledge of the magazine industry and she feels she can adapt to working in it.

Never Say: "I think it will be fine." This candidate needs to explain why she feels that way.

Q What do you know about some of our major clients?

A I know your major clients are all in the canned food industry. BBR represents Heller Foods, Green Products, and Acorn Corp. I read in *Advertising Digest* just last week that Heans hired you to run their new broadcast campaign.

This candidate has done his homework, even keeping up with the latest industry news.

Never Say: "I haven't had a chance to find out who they are." There is never an excuse for not attempting to learn what you can about a prospective employer.

Essential

When a prospective employer asks you to describe your dream job, choose one on your career path. You don't want to describe a job that is unrelated to the one for which you are applying. The job you describe should also be several rungs above your current one on the career ladder. Show how you want your career to progress.

Q Describe your ideal job.

A Ideally, I'd like to work as a senior project manager overseeing the development of housing complexes.

Through her research this candidate has learned the job for which she is interviewing will eventually lead to the one she is describing. She demonstrates that she will be loyal to the company if it hires her.

Never Say: "I'd love to teach one day." It's nice to have career aspirations, but they should at least be related to the job you are applying for.

Q Describe your ideal company to work for.

A I'd like to work for a software company where I will have the opportunity to contribute to the business by utilizing my programming skills as well as my teaching abilities.

When describing his ideal company, this applicant speaks in terms of what he can bring to it. Any company is ideal to him if he can use his skills to benefit it, he seems to be saying. Having done his homework, he knows he is describing the company at which he is interviewing.

Never Say: "I'd really like to work for a big company but none of them are hiring right now." Honesty isn't always the best policy.

Q Our latest venture has been all over the news. What would you do to make the transition go more smoothly for our employees?

A I would make sure employees know how the merger between this company and Pacific Pencil Company will affect them. I would hold meetings to discuss how procedures will change and schedule workshops to help employees adapt to these changes. When my former employer merged with RQR International, I assisted the vice president who was responsible for handling the transition, so I have experience in this area.

By referring to the venture by name, this candidate shows she knows what the interviewer is talking about. She has clearly given some thought to how this merger will affect the company and knows how to deal with it, and she draws upon her experience with a similar situation.

Never Say: "What venture is that? I haven't had time lately to pay attention to the news."

Q Can you define this position as you understand it?

A This position involves supervising a staff of about fifty-five data entry clerks. I would be responsible for scheduling employees, delegating work assignments, and quality control.

This candidate understands the job for which he is interviewing. He has read the job announcement and has listened carefully during the interview.

Never Say: "Data entry supervisor." It's good that the candidate at least knows the title of the job he is interviewing for. However, it's not good enough. He needs to elaborate if possible.

 **Question**

What should I do if I don't know much about the job for which I'm applying?
Sometimes employers release little information about open positions. If the interviewer asks you what you know about the job but you haven't managed to find many details, say so. You can tell her what you know so far and use this opportunity to ask for a better description.

Q Are you available during the hours we're open?

A Yes, I am. I took a look at your website and saw that the library provides service Monday through Saturday from 9 A.M. to 9 P.M. I'm available during all those times.

This interviewee knows what the hours are and can commit to working when he is needed.

Never Say: "What hours are you open?" The candidate should have been able to find this information.

Q You are aware you will have to relocate to this city if we hire you. Do you think you will like living here?

A I've done some research about this city and I think it would be a great place to live. The crime rate is pretty low and the climate is just about perfect. There are so many museums and theaters here, it won't be hard to find something to do on my time off.

This answer proves that this candidate has done her research and learned as much as she could about this city. She is prepared to make a well-informed decision if the employer offers her the job.

Never Say: "I can be happy anywhere." This interviewee may show that she is flexible, but since she didn't do any research into moving to a new location, this prospective employer may not see her as someone who is committed to making a permanent move.

Alert

An employer should not ask if you are unable to work on a particular day due to religious observance. The Civil Rights Act of 1964 prohibits employment discrimination on the basis of religion. If you can't work on a particular day, hold off on having this discussion until you have received a job offer.

Q I see from your resume that you were a member of Students Against Teen Smoking. Since one of the largest tobacco companies is our major client, will your antismoking stance pose a problem for you when dealing with this company?

A When I first discovered that Wyatt and Smokey Incorporated was one of Krull Media's clients, I hesitated to apply. I decided to do some research to learn more about W & S and found out that the company has never marketed its product to teens or tried to make it appealing to them in any way. Actually, I saw the company ran a campaign last year that addressed the issue of underage smoking. I understand your agency worked on that campaign.

This candidate did research in order to learn about his prospective employer. In doing so, he learned that he might have philosophical differences with one of the employer's clients. Not wanting to compromise his principles or take himself out of the running for the job, he did further research to help him learn more about the client in question.

Never Say: "I had no idea one of this company's clients was a tobacco company." Had this candidate known that, he would have been able to make an educated decision about whether to even interview for the job. He might be wasting the interviewer's time.

Q Do you know who our major competitors are?

A Yes, I do. There are four big names in the communications industry. There's BCD, DRG, Parrot, and of course, this company, Chime.

This candidate couldn't have answered this question had she not done her homework.

Never Say: "Nope."

Q Would you rather be a big fish in a small pond or a small fish in a big pond?

A I would much rather be a big fish in a small pond. Working for a small company provides me with the opportunity to use more of my skills. I like it when my job duties are diversified. Most of my experience has been with small companies, so I understand the unique challenges that can come up. For example, I know how to be careful when scheduling out-of-town business meetings so there are always enough people in the office to deal with emergencies that come up.

This candidate is interviewing for a job in a small company. He explains why this is a better fit for him.

Never Say: "Whichever." This candidate should use this opportunity to explain why he is a good fit for this employer.

Q What do you think will be different about working for this company than working for your current employer?

A My current employer sells home furnishings, while this company sells office furnishings. This means I will work with a different group of clients and new products; however, I can utilize my skills as a decorator and as a salesperson here as I do with my current employer.

This candidate knows enough about her prospective employer to answer this question. She makes a point of discussing how her skills can be used to work with a different product and different clientele.

Never Say: "It's a much shorter commute." This may be true, but it doesn't really have much to do with what this candidate can bring to her prospective employer.

Q How well do you understand our mission?

A From my research, I understand your mission is to develop high-quality toys that enhance learning and provide entertainment for children between preschool and ten years of age.

This candidate states the company's mission as he understands it, which is exactly what the interviewer asked him to do.

Never Say: "Well . . . I know you sell toys." While you may not always be able to find out what a company's mission is, you should at least try to do the research.

Q If you were interviewing potential employees for a job here, how would you describe this organization to them?

A XRT, Inc. manufactures windows and sells them directly to the consumer. The company has a sales force of about twenty people who respond to customer inquiries by visiting their homes or places of business.

This answer shows that this interviewee has a firm grasp of what this business is all about.

Never Say: "It's a window company in Chicago." This answer doesn't prove this candidate knows much about this company.

Q If you had the opportunity to develop a new product to add to our line, what would it be?

A Since Perfect Posies currently sells flowers and other gift items, I think a line of chocolate would be a good choice. I recently saw a survey that said that consumers spend $150 billion on chocolate gifts each year, so this would be a great market to enter. And since this company already has a great reputation in the mail-order gift industry and the systems in place to handle the addition of this product, this would be a natural expansion of Perfect Posies' product line.

This is an extremely well-thought-out answer based on this candidate's knowledge of the company and the gift industry in general.

Never Say: "I don't know much about your current line. Do you offer anything besides flowers yet?"

Chapter 10

What Would You Do If You Were Hired?

WHEN A PROSPECTIVE employer looks at you, she sees you in three ways—past, present, and future. Your work history and your education make up your past. Your personality, strengths and weaknesses, and skills make up your present, or who you are today. Finally, a prospective employer wants to know the future— that is, what you would do if she hires you. Without a crystal ball, she must ask a lot of questions in order to get a clearer picture of who you are.

What You Can Bring to the Company

The interviewer's primary concern is to find out if you will be able to carry out the duties of the job. In most situations, you will have had the opportunity to read a job description in advance of your interview. If not, try your best to determine what the typical job duties are for the position you are applying for. You should be ready to explain why you are qualified to carry out each duty.

A prospective employer might talk about some specific projects he has in store for his new hire. He will want you to discuss how you will approach those projects. This would be a good time for you to talk about how you approached similar projects in the past. The interviewer may also present a number of hypothetical situations and ask you to explain how you will handle them. Whenever possible, draw on your past experiences to illustrate how your skills will enable you to deal with each situation.

E ssential

Arm yourself with a cache of examples that best illustrate that you are the most qualified candidate for the job. These examples will come from your work experience and, in lieu of that, from your experience as a student, whether in class or through your participation in extracurricular activities.

What the Company Expects of You

Every employer has different expectations for her employees. While one might require you to work long hours on a regular basis, another might expect you to work late occasionally, perhaps during a particular busy season. Some jobs involve frequent travel. For other jobs you must be on call during weekends. The interviewer will try to determine whether you can meet a particular job requirement by asking you direct and indirect questions about it.

It is in your best interests to be honest about what you are willing to do regarding traveling and working late. If you know you must pay your dues and will be amenable to doing whatever your boss asks of you, then by all means indicate that during the interview. However, if you are not, you should let the employer know right away. It is always best to be up front and not create false expectations.

A job interview is about more than the employer deciding whether he should hire you. You can use the information you gather to decide whether the company is a good fit for you. You will be able to learn about the demands of the job from some of the interviewer's questions. You may uncover a deal-breaker that was not mentioned in the job description. For example, when an interviewer asks if working late is a problem for you, that indicates the employer will probably expect you to do that. If you can't or don't want to, this is probably not a good place for you to work. You should consider yourself lucky to have learned this now rather than further along in the hiring process, or even worse, once you have accepted a job offer. If extenuating circumstances prevent you from fulfilling a certain job requirement, for example, if you can't work late because of another obligation but you can come in early and are willing to do so, let the interviewer know. Your prospective employer may be able to work within the parameters of your schedule.

Alert

If an interviewer asks you about your willingness or ability to travel or to work late, saying you can't do it will probably take you out of the running for the job. With that in mind, speak up only if you are positive that you are not able or willing to do something. However, if you don't speak up during the interview, you must do so before accepting a job offer.

In addition to trying to learn what you will bring to the company, a prospective employer may also want to find out what you expect to get from it, particularly your salary requirements. If possible, avoid discussing salary during a job interview, or at least during a first interview. That topic is best put off until you are closer to receiving an offer. If the interviewer asks what salary you are looking for, attempt to turn the question around on him by asking what salary they are offering. If that doesn't work, talk about the typical salary range in your field, leaving an extensive discussion of specifics for later.

Questions and Answers

Q The department you would be in charge of hasn't had a supervisor in months. This is going to be a big transition for the staff. How will you handle it?

A I wouldn't want to make any big changes for at least the first two weeks. I find it's better to just observe how things are done before trying to make any improvements. I want to gain the staff's trust first and listen to their concerns.

This candidate has a plan in place and she lays it out step by step. She knows that employees who have been unsupervised for a long time need to get used to having someone overseeing their work.

Never Say: "Well, the first thing I would do is make some changes around here. If there hasn't been a supervisor running things for a while, things are sure to be messed up." This is not a well-thought-out answer and could indicate that the applicant might make impulsive decisions.

Q The person who fills this position will have to work on his own most of the time. Can you handle that?

A I am used to working independently. On my last job, I edited the company newsletter. I was responsible for compiling the material, writing the articles, and preparing the newsletter for publication each quarter. I had to set my own deadlines for each step along the way.

This candidate explains how a project he was responsible for prepared him to work independently.

Never Say: "I love working on my own. It's less distracting." This answer shows that this candidate may be able to work on his own, but he's inflexible. If he had to work with others, could he?

Q How do you feel about working long hours?

A Can you explain what you mean by long hours? Does that mean working late or getting to work early?

The applicant knows she already has a commitment two nights a week. She doesn't mind getting to work early, though. She decides it's better to find out what her prospective employer's expectations are before she rules anything out or commits to something with which she won't be able to follow through.

Never Say: "I love working long hours. It means I don't have to go home and deal with my family." Even if the applicant is trying to be funny, this is not the place to bring up personal issues.

 **Question**

What should I do if I don't understand a question?
If you don't understand what the interviewer is asking you or you just need something clarified, it's okay to ask questions during the interview. It is preferable to giving a response that doesn't answer the question.

Q We're kind of casual here. I see you've worn a suit today. How would you dress for work if I hire you?

A I would adhere to the culture of this company and would dress in slacks and a nice shirt.

This candidate knows it's important to fit in with the culture of the workplace. Only after a quick assessment of the interviewer's attire does he go on with the second part of his answer.

Never Say: "I feel more comfortable in a suit." Perhaps he would feel more comfortable elsewhere.

Q Senior citizens represent a huge market now and we want to convince them to buy our product. If we hired you, how would you help with that?

A In addition to being a very big market, the senior market is also a growing market. They are a group with a very active lifestyle. Many have expendable income and they choose to use their savings on travel, so it's clear we have a product they will want. We have to determine how to reach them. I would first do research to find out what publications seniors read and what television shows they watch. Only then can we embark on an advertising campaign.

This candidate demonstrates the methodical approach she would take. She shows her understanding of the market.

Never Say: "Seniors don't have a lot of money to spend, so why would we target them?" This interviewee doesn't know the market and contradicts the interviewer.

Q We're about to change over to a new software program for our shipping and receiving department. We'd like the person we hire for this position to do the training. Are you the right person for that job?

A I am definitely the right person for this job. As you can see on my resume, my last job was with a software distributor. One of my responsibilities was to travel to our clients' offices to provide software training.

This is one confident candidate who clearly illustrates he has the skills the company is seeking.

Never Say: "Um, I did some training." This applicant doesn't sound very confident.

Q In about a year we want to open a new branch on the other side of town. We plan to train the person who takes this position to run that office. Is that something you'd be interested in?

A I would welcome that opportunity if it arises.

Notice the applicant says, "If it arises." She wants to express her eagerness to take on more responsibility with this employer without sounding like she'd leave if that opportunity doesn't come up or if such an opportunity comes up sooner with another company.

Never Say: "That's exactly what I'm looking for." Since the candidate only just learned of these plans, how can a job running a new but currently nonexistent office be exactly what she's looking for? What about the job for which she's currently interviewing?

Q If we hire you, will you be willing to get your certification? You have all the skills we're looking for, but we really need someone who is certified.

A I was planning to take my certification exam in June. That's the next time it's being given.

While it would have been okay for this candidate to say he would get his certification because the prospective employer has asked him to, it's even better that he said he was planning to do it anyway.

Never Say: "I don't understand why certification matters so much, but if you need me to do it I will." Show some enthusiasm, please.

Q The person who last held this position took ill and has only been able to work off and on for the last three months. Last month he resigned. Things are a huge mess, which the person we hire will need to sort out. Are you up for the challenge?

A I love a good challenge. First I'll sort through the mess to organize it. Then I'll see which things require immediate attention and which things I can work on later.

The interviewee, by giving this answer, shows that she knows how to both organize and prioritize. These are two skills that are extremely important for someone taking over a job that has been neglected.

Never Say: "I'm sure once I see the mess I can figure out what to do with it." Even though this candidate shows confidence, she doesn't present a plan.

Q The person we hire will have to respond to customer complaints occasionally. Will you be able to do that?

A Years ago I worked in customer service. I'll be able to put that experience to good use.

The interviewee finds some past experience that will help him with this aspect of the job.

Never Say: "I'm sure it won't be too big a deal." If the interviewer bothered to ask this question, it may, in fact, be a big deal.

Q We often work on teams here. Would you rather work on a team or on your own?

A I work well both independently and on a team. In my previous jobs I had to do both. We often worked on teams to complete larger projects. I like how working on a team allows you to draw on the strength of each of its members.

This interviewee shows she is flexible enough to work on either a team or independently but addresses the focus of the question by emphasizing her teamwork skills.

Never Say: "On a team, of course." This candidate just says what she thinks the interviewer wants to hear without giving any proof to back up her answer.

Q We have several clients with outstanding bills. If we hire you, how will you handle this situation?

A First, I would want to go through the paperwork to make sure these clients were properly notified their accounts are delinquent. If I find out they were notified, I'll call each one personally to discuss this. There might be extenuating circumstances. It's important not to be too heavy-handed in dealing with these types of situations. After all, these are our clients. We don't want to lose them entirely.

This candidate gives a clearly thought-out answer illustrating that he knows how important it is to be diplomatic when dealing with clients.

Never Say: "My first priority would be getting on the phone and getting payment from them as quickly as possible." While this might work, it would also alienate clients.

Q Our clients expect a very quick turnaround on the projects we do for them. Can you handle that?

A Yes, I can. While I was in graduate school, I had several professors who assigned projects that were due only a few days later. I became an expert at scheduling my time around completing these assignments.

Since this interviewee doesn't have work experience to draw upon, she talks about her experience as a student. In the process she highlights a valuable skill—time management.

Never Say: "I'm sure I can." This interviewee needs to give a specific example or, in the absence of one, talk about any skills she possesses that will help her.

Q If you are hired for this position, you will go from managing your current staff of ten to managing fifty people. Will you be able to oversee a substantially larger staff?

A Yes, I will. Although I've never managed a staff of that size before, I know I have the skills necessary to do it. I am a strong leader. I am good at communicating with my staff so that each member knows what he or she needs to accomplish. I am also adept at delegating responsibilities, which will be even more important with such a large staff.

This candidate lets the interviewer know that he has all the skills that a good manager should have, even though he doesn't have experience with the exact situation he will face.

Never Say: "Since I've never managed such a big staff, I might find it overwhelming. I'm sure I'll be able to handle it, though." This interviewee focuses on the negative rather than on why he can handle the job despite his lack of experience. He should never mention feeling overwhelmed.

Q We're implementing a new computer system in this department. If we hire you for this position, you'll need to spend a month in Seattle learning how to use it. Are you okay with that?

A That would be fine.

This is a yes or no question. The interviewee doesn't need to say any more than this. However, if the answer is "no" she will need to provide an explanation.

Never Say: "That sounds great, but do you know when that would be? It rains a lot in Seattle and I hate the rain. Don't you?" This candidate has said way too much.

Q When we are in the process of developing a new product, it's essential that information about it doesn't leak out. How are you at keeping secrets?

A After working in the technology field for the last three years, I know how important it is to keep information confidential until a product is released.

This candidate demonstrates that confidentiality has not been a problem for him in the past.

Never Say: "Wouldn't I have to sign a confidentiality agreement or something?" Is threat of being sued for breach of contract the only thing that would keep this applicant quiet?

 Fact

Companies are always racing to release new products before the competition. They expect their employees to keep any information they learn about the new product behind company doors. You may be asked questions about your ability to adhere to such a requirement.

Q We currently have several employees who have problems with things like tardiness and excessive personal phone calls. How would you deal with this if we hired you as supervisor?

A First, I would need to find out exactly what is happening. Then, prior to singling out any one employee, I would circulate a memo to the entire department that reiterated the rules. If the behavior continued, I would have a private meeting with each employee who isn't following the rules. I would stress the importance of following the rules and try to find out if there are extenuating circumstances that could be remedied. If the employee continues to break the rules, there would be repercussions.

This interviewee is clearly not one to leap without looking. She knows how important it is to evaluate a situation before taking action. However, she will take action in an expedient manner.

Never Say: "You won't have to worry about anyone breaking the rules once I take over." This candidate must put forth a series of steps she will take to remedy the situation.

Q Four times a year we work around the clock for about a week. Will that be a problem?

A That's fine with me. I understand the beginning of each season is a very busy time.

Not only is this job candidate willing to work late, he knows enough about the industry to know what times of year this would be expected of him.

Never Say: "Do you let people take vacation during those times?" He hasn't even started and he sounds like he's trying to wiggle out of responsibility.

Q As my assistant, would I be able to trust you to take over for me whenever I'm out of the office?

A Absolutely. I would follow whatever rules you set forth. I also have excellent judgment, so I can handle whatever comes up.

The applicant uses this opportunity to highlight her skills.

Never Say: "Does that happen a lot?" This answer makes the applicant seem unsure of whether she can handle this responsibility.

Q Whoever fills this position will need to write next year's budget, which needs to be 10 percent lower than the current one. Could you do this?

A I had to do something similar when my department went through funding cuts last year and I was in charge of writing the new budget. First I reviewed the current year's budget and removed amounts that had been budgeted for one-time events. Then I found a few areas where our actual expenditures were lower than we had budgeted for, and I was able to bring the amount down to more realistic levels, of course accounting for possible price increases. Finally, I went through it to see what cuts would have a minimal effect on services. I cut a program that traditionally had very low attendance. This eliminated the need to hire a part-time instructor. I was able to submit a budget that was 12 percent lower than the one for the previous year.

This candidate demonstrates how he takes a practical approach to trimming a budget. He shows how he is able to get the job done with a minimal effect on service.

Never Say: "Some of the budget cuts I make may be unpopular, but saving the agency money is my priority." It's true that saving money is important. However, there are consequences of making radical cuts that will affect service.

Q This job requires some travel. Is that a problem?

A I understand that traveling is common in this industry and that's fine with me. I look forward to representing this company around the country.

This candidate has done her homework and wisely speaks of herself as if she has the job.

Never Say: "I love traveling. There are so many places I want to visit." This candidate's mistake is talking about how she will benefit from traveling rather than talking about how her trips will benefit her prospective employer.

Q The students in this school can be very challenging to manage. As a teacher here, will you be able to handle them?

A I worked with special needs children when I was an assistant teacher at Ardsley School. I learned it is important to look at each child as an individual. Each one has different strengths and weaknesses. If you look at it that way, you can figure out what strategy you need to use to work with each child. Children will trust you when they know you see them as individuals and will usually respond by doing what you need them to do.

Although this candidate is applying for his first professional job, he is able to draw on past experience. He explains what he learned from his previous experience as an assistant teacher.

Never Say: "I'm a strict disciplinarian, so this won't be a problem." This answer doesn't demonstrate that this interviewee has a strategy for dealing with difficult children.

Q Anyone who takes this position will need to handle stress well. Are you good at handling stress?

A Yes, I am. My last job was very stressful, but I found that practicing some relaxation techniques like deep breathing helped me combat the stress. I also made sure to take a lunch break every day, since that gives me time to regroup and start the rest of my day with a positive attitude.

This candidate demonstrates that she has strategies in place to help her deal with stress.

Never Say: "If you love your job, you don't find it stressful." That is unrealistic. Even if you love your job, it can be stressful at times. Those who have a coping mechanism will be better able to deal with stressful situations.

Q In this fast-paced environment we need someone who can think on his feet. Are you that person?

A Yes, I am. I have experience making thoughtful decisions under pressure. I worked at a daily newspaper for five years. Every day we had to make last-minute decisions about what to include in the next day's edition. There was no time to waste when the paper had to go to press within the next half-hour.

This candidate shows how his experience has taught him how to be decisive.

Never Say: "Uhm . . . well, let me think about this. . . . Let's see . . . hmm . . ." This candidate's hesitation says more than any answer could.

Q Each employee in this department is on call one weekend a month. How do you feel about that?

A That is fine with me.

The candidate gives a succinct answer, which is all that is needed here.

Never Say: "Would I get paid for being on call?" That question can wait until a job offer is made and salary is negotiated.

Q Are you willing to work late occasionally?

A I know what it's like when a deadline is coming up. In my last job I was asked to work late from time to time. It was never a problem for me. When a deadline is quickly approaching, I'll be able to make sure we meet it.

By giving this answer, the interviewee not only uses language that lets the interviewer visualize her in the position for which she's interviewing, but also tells her prospective boss that she's worked late in the past.

Never Say: "I'll work late every night if you want me to." Is this interviewee just saying what she thinks the interviewer wants to hear?

 **Question**

What should I do if I can't work on a particular day because of my religious beliefs?
If you can't work on a particular day because of your religious beliefs, tell your prospective employer you'd be happy to make up the time on another day. Remember, an employer must reasonably accommodate employees' sincerely held religious beliefs and cannot base a hiring decision on this.

Q As a contact person for our clients, part of your job is keeping them calm. That sometimes means

not sharing inconsequential details with them. For example, we never would want a client to know about a small mishap that occurred with a project we were working on for them as long as it was resolved and didn't cause any real problems. Would you be comfortable with that?

A I'm always inclined to be honest but I would always do my best to preserve our relationships with our clients. As long as there was no long-term damage that would reveal itself at a later date, I'm well aware that our clients don't need to know everything that goes on when we are working on their project. No need to worry anyone unnecessarily. Of course, I will work to make sure the problem is resolved as quickly as possible.

Knowing what common practice is in his field helps this candidate answer this question. He know that withholding some information— as long as it isn't damaging in the long run—is okay.

Never Say: "I never ever tell lies, so I can't not tell our clients everything. It's wrong." This candidate may not know the field well enough to give the correct answer. While it may sound virtuous to never tell lies, he doesn't realize that some things shouldn't be shared outside the company for which he works.

Q It's getting too expensive to operate a business in this city. Would you be willing to relocate?

A I'd be willing to relocate anywhere within the United States.

This candidate gives an honest answer.

Never Say: "I love to move around, so that's really good news." This applicant's answer alludes to the fact that stability isn't his strong suit.

Q What salary are you looking for?

A From my research, I know the salary range for those with my experience working in this industry here in New York is $51,000 to $55,000 per year. I'm confident we can agree on a salary that is acceptable.

This applicant has done her homework. She gives a range rather than an absolute number, showing her flexibility.

Never Say: "I have to make $52,000 per year." One should always avoid giving an absolute number when discussing salary on a job interview.

Q I see from the salary history you sent that you were earning $45,000 on your last job. We've taken some losses over the last year and won't be able to pay you that. Will that be a problem?

A I'm sure we can agree on a reasonable salary.

This applicant knows it's better to discuss salary after the employer makes an offer.

Never Say: "How much less than that will it be?" Don't make the employer think you're only in it for the money. The salary discussion should wait until later.

Chapter 11

Difficult or Embarrassing Questions

DO YOU DREAD going on job interviews because you are afraid the interviewer will ask you about a situation you find embarrassing or difficult to explain? Were you fired from your last job or is there a huge gap in your work history? The interviewer is likely to notice any gaps or inconsistencies on your resume, so you need to be prepared to answer the questions of which you are most afraid. Here are strategies for coping with that aspect of job interviewing.

I Hope They Don't Ask Me That

When a prospective employer reviews your resume, he will look for things like lengthy gaps between jobs or jobs that don't fit in with the rest of your experience. He will also notice if you hopped around from job to job or if you had a series of jobs that didn't move in an upward direction. An employer will probably question why you were at a job for a short period of time; or he may question why you have been with one employer for your entire career.

An interviewer may ask questions about your lack of experience if he feels you haven't been in the field for very long. If you appear to be overqualified for the job, the interviewer will question you about that as well. If you don't have the formal education that is called for, you will probably be asked to explain why. If your education is in one area and the job you are interviewing for is in another, the interviewer will inquire about that, too.

E ssential

An interviewer will ask you to discuss things he can't ascertain from reading your resume. While your resume gives the period of time you worked at every job, it doesn't show why you left each one. A prospective employer will want to know about that. He may also ask you to discuss your relationships with supervisors and coworkers.

How to Answer Difficult Questions

When you answer difficult questions, be honest. Don't make excuses for things, and do not lie. For example, if you got fired from a job, don't tell the interviewer you quit. She can learn the truth from a simple call to your former employer or through a background check, so you are better off being up front no matter how embarrassed you feel. The interviewer will appreciate your candor. If you lie, you will have two strikes against you. Not only will a prospective employer know you got fired, but you will have shown her you are dishonest. Don't place blame on your former employer or speak negatively about him. When possible, highlight the positive and talk about what you have done to overcome whatever it is that put a blemish on your past.

If an employer asks about a gap in employment, be honest about why it's there. Discuss things you did during that time to enhance your skills. For example, if you took time off to be at home with young children, talk about how you kept up with your career by reading professional literature and taking classes. If you didn't give much thought to your career during that time, or have decided to enter a new field, talk about how you are preparing now for your return to work.

Address concerns about your lack of education or experience by explaining what you've done to compensate for it. If your experience makes up for your lack of a formal degree, say so and explain how this is the case. If you plan to take some courses to enhance your skills, elaborate on that. Remember to be specific when you discuss your plans.

If you were fired from a previous job, you may be concerned that revealing that information will take you out of the running for a job, but don't try to hide it. The prospective employer will probably want to talk to your prior boss before she hires you. When she does, she will learn the truth.

Question

The word "fired" sounds so bad. Is there something I can say instead?
You don't have to use the word "fired" to say you had to leave a job. It has a negative connotation, as does "terminated" or "dismissed." You can say you had a "parting of the ways" or a "disagreement," which basically means the same thing but doesn't sound as harsh.

If you have been job-hunting for a while, you are probably concerned that a prospective employer will wonder why. You can blame the economy if the current one is bad. Even if the general economy is good, the market for someone with your skills may not be. Make sure the market really is bad; you don't want to infer that you don't understand the industry. State your skills and say that you haven't been able to find a job where those skills are needed.

Questions and Answers

Q You were at your last job for only six months. Why were you there for such a short time?

A Unfortunately, the job turned out to be much different from what I thought it would be. It's a good thing I discovered this early on before the employer invested more time in me and I invested more time in the company. I know I could put my editing skills to much better use in this position.

Notice the interviewer places no blame on either himself or his employer. He doesn't say the employer didn't tell him the truth about the job or that he misunderstood what he'd be doing. He also shows how he looked out for both his employer and himself by leaving before more time was invested.

Never Say: "My boss blatantly lied to me during the interview. The job turned out to be very different from what she told me." This candidate's mistake was speaking poorly of his boss.

Alert

Keep your negativity in check when you talk about a former employer. No matter how much you hate him, keep your feelings to yourself. Speak poorly of your former boss and a prospective employer will wonder if someday you will speak poorly of her.

Q What do your subordinates think of you?

A They think I'm a tough boss. I expect a lot out of them.

This candidate, by giving this succinct answer, provides just enough information to answer the question. He makes no indication of whether his subordinates like him or not.

Never Say: "I'm a tough boss and because of that my subordinates resent me." This interviewee has said more than he needs to.

Q I see from your resume that you've had five jobs in five years. Why have you moved around so much?

A When I first graduated from college, I wasn't sure what I wanted to do. After trying out several jobs, I have come to the conclusion that this field is the right one for me. I even took some courses to enhance my skills. I know I can do a good job here.

This is an honest answer. The candidate states that she has figured out what she wants to do and is now committed to this field. She then goes on to prove it by talking about how she is enhancing her skills.

Never Say: "I can't stay in one place for too long. . . . I mean, I couldn't stay in one place too long. Now I can." The candidate can't keep her answers straight. Is her need to move around still a problem? This interviewer is sure to be suspicious.

Q You've been out of the job market for the last six years. Can you explain that, please?

A I took a hiatus from the workforce to raise my children. I am now ready to come back and use my skills. I have kept up with developments in the field during my absence by reading professional literature and attending seminars.

This candidate doesn't make excuses for his time away from the workforce. He does make a point of letting the employer know he didn't lose track of his career during this time.

Never Say: "I was busy raising my family, but I can't afford to stay home anymore." This doesn't let the employer know that this candidate is ready to return to the workforce and wants to do that, only that he needs to. The interviewer will wonder if this candidate will stop working should his financial situation change.

Q According to your resume, you were a manager at Crane Computer Store from 1990 through 1995 and then assistant manager at a different branch of the store starting in 1995. Were you demoted?

A This wasn't a demotion. I was originally manager of the paper products department. It was a very small section. When an opening came up for an assistant manager in the home PC department at another store, I jumped at the chance. It was a much better opportunity because it was a much larger department and I knew I would have greater responsibilities.

Although her job title would indicate this candidate had been demoted, she explains why this wasn't actually the case. She was willing to trade the manager title for a job with more responsibility. If she had been demoted, however, she would need to explain why.

Never Say: "I didn't want all the responsibility of being a manager." Should this candidate really say she doesn't want a job with responsibility?

Q Why did you leave Community Publications Corporation?

A My boss and I had a difference of opinion and we decided it would be best if I left my job.

The interviewee decides to be honest about his reasons for leaving his job. He doesn't blame his boss or berate himself, but simply tells the truth about being fired.

Never Say: "That idiot fired me." Making disparaging comments about your boss is a poor choice.

Q Tell me how your career progressed at your last job.

A I was hired as assistant to the staff accountant. When she left, I was asked to take her position. After three months, my boss and I decided that I didn't yet have the skills for such a demanding job after all, and I stepped back into the assistant position when they hired someone with more experience. That was three years ago, and I now have the experience I needed back then.

The candidate gives an honest answer. He explains that his "backward" progress from accountant to assistant was due to his lack of experience. He claims that he now has the experience to be a staff accountant.

Never Say: "They promoted me before I was ready and then when they found someone they liked better, they sent me back to my original job." This answer makes the candidate sound very bitter about what happened. He also doesn't say anything about the skills he currently has.

Q If I asked your previous supervisor for a reference, how would she describe you?

A My supervisor and I often disagreed about many things. One thing we would agree on, I think, is that I did my job well.

This candidate is in a tricky situation. He and his supervisor didn't get along well, but that doesn't mean he wasn't a good employee. He gives this answer hoping his former boss will put their differences aside and be honest about his performance at work if she is called as a reference.

Never Say: "She probably has nothing nice to say. She's always had it in for me." This candidate doesn't give his supervisor a chance to say something bad about him—he does it himself.

Q Your resume says that you are an administrative assistant, yet you're applying for a job that has much more responsibility. What makes you think you can handle it?

A Even though my job title is administrative assistant, I have many more responsibilities than that title usually implies. I train all new support staff and supervise junior clerks.

This answer explains how this candidate's responsibilities differed from what one might assume from her job title. She chooses to discuss the aspects of her current job that are related to the job for which she is interviewing.

Never Say: "Even though I was technically an administrative assistant, I did a lot of other stuff." The candidate needs to be more specific and explain what that "other stuff" was in order to demonstrate she has experience handling the responsibilities she would have on the job for which she is interviewing.

Q You seem to be overqualified for this position. Why do you want this job?

A I definitely bring a lot of skills to this job. I look forward to using my experience to help your company grow.

Rather than downplay his skills in response to what the interviewer has said, this candidate chooses to talk about how his experience and skills will benefit the company.

Never Say: "I don't really have that much experience." A job candidate should never make less of his skills, regardless of what the interviewer thinks.

Q There's a ten-year gap in your employment history. What were you doing during that time?

A I was convicted of theft and was incarcerated at the state penitentiary from 1989 through 1999. During that time I earned a degree in social work that I want to use in working with young people who may be headed in the wrong direction.

A conviction will show up when the employer does a background check on this candidate, so it makes no sense for her to lie. She makes a point of discussing why she is qualified for the job for which she has applied.

Never Say: "I took some time off from the workforce." The employer may hire the candidate in spite of a prior conviction, especially if she shows that she has turned her life around. However, if she lies about the conviction and the employer finds out the truth, she probably won't get the job.

Q Have you ever been convicted of a felony?

A Yes, I have. I served three years for a hit and run. I finished my college courses while I was in jail.

This candidate gives an honest answer and hopes it won't affect his chances of being hired. Generally, the interviewer can ask if a job candidate has ever been convicted of a felony.

Never Say: "Why? Are you going to do a background check?" The employer will certainly do a background check after hearing that response or she may simply decide to take this candidate out of consideration for the job.

Q In your first job out of college you worked as a receptionist. Weren't you a little overqualified?

A My education did overqualify me for that job, but I was determined to work in the advertising industry. I knew if I took that job, it would give me the chance to show off my skills. I volunteered to do some proofreading for the copywriter, and after six months he asked me to be his assistant.

This candidate shows the interviewer that she knew what she had to do to reach her goals. She also tells the interviewer that her plan worked.

Never Say: "It was the only thing available." This applicant did not have a clear goal in mind when she took the job.

Q On your resume you indicated that you attended Harkin College for a few years, but I don't see a degree listed. Did you graduate?

A No, I didn't graduate. I withdrew from the college during my junior year. I decided that I wasn't getting as much out of college as I should have, so I decided to go to work. I plan to continue my education in the future.

This is an honest answer. The candidate takes responsibility for discontinuing his formal education and expresses his desire to complete his education.

Never Say: "The school was horrible. I didn't want to waste my parents' money." If this was the real reason this job candidate dropped out of school he probably would have finished his education elsewhere.

Q What were your grades like in college?

A My grades could have been better. If I had it to do over again, I would have studied a lot harder than I did.

The candidate doesn't blame anyone but herself for her poor grades and makes a point of saying she would do things differently now.

Never Say: "They were okay." If the candidate did poorly in school she should admit it. If the employer asks for a copy of her college transcript, which he might, the candidate will be caught in a lie. Furthermore, having described her poor grades as "okay," the interviewer may question why the applicant's expectations are so low she thinks earning bad grades is okay.

 Fact

In 2005, 12 percent of wage and salary workers in the United States was between the ages of fifty-five and sixty-four, and almost 3 percent was age sixty-five or older, according to the U.S. Census Bureau. The Bureau of Labor Statistics reports employment of workers age sixty-five and older increased 101 percent in the thirty years between 1977 and 2007.

Q If we hire you, the person who will be your supervisor is much younger than you are. Will this be a problem for you?

A If she has the skills necessary to be a supervisor, I will be happy to work for her.

This candidate gives a straightforward answer to this question. He does not know whether the interviewer is concerned about whether he will not be able to take direction from someone younger than he or if the interviewer is implying the candidate is too old for the job. The applicant chooses to ignore the implication that he is too old and instead addresses the interviewers concern about his ability to take direction from a younger supervisor.

Never Say: "Are you implying that I'm old?" The candidate is much too confrontational, which will turn the interviewer off regardless of what her question implies.

Q I see you left your last job about eight months ago. Have you been looking for work since then? Can you explain that?

A Yes, I have been looking for a job for the last several months. I am skilled in technical support, system design and implementation, and training. I haven't been able to find a position for someone with my skills.

This candidate gives an honest answer to the question. He states his skills and then explains that the job market has been tight for someone with those skills. Since he has no control over the job market, he doesn't have to make excuses for it.

Never Say: "I know if I had looked harder for a job, I would have found one. After all, I have great skills." The candidate may think it's better to say he couldn't find a job because he wasn't looking for one, but this answer only shows his lack of motivation.

Q Why are you applying for a job outside the subject in which you majored?

A I can use the skills I developed as a psychology major to succeed in marketing research. I have taken courses in consumer behavior, statistics, and research design, which I know will be useful in this field.

This candidate shows how her skills are transferable to this field. If she plans to further pursue a career in psychology, she doesn't imply it by giving this answer.

Never Say: "I need to work to save up money for graduate school." The employer has good reason to wonder how long this person will stay if he hires her.

Q You don't seem to have a great deal of work experience. Why should we hire you?

A I may not have a lot of paid work experience, but I have a lot of volunteer experience. I organized a voter registration drive in my community and registered 300 new voters during the last election. For the past four years I have chaired the committee that runs the book fair at my son's school. We have raised more than $7,000 each year.

While this candidate doesn't have paid work experience, she has been able to hone her skills through her volunteer work. She has persuaded people to register to vote and worked on a committee that successfully ran a major fundraising event. She even gives dollar amounts to back up her claims.

Never Say: "I really want this job, and I know I will be good at it." This candidate needs to tell the interviewer what skills she has and how she will use them to benefit his company.

Q Aren't you underqualified for this job?

A I don't think I am. While it's true I don't have a lot of experience yet, I do have very good skills, as we discussed earlier. I am willing to learn any additional skills I need to have to do this job.

The candidate doesn't try to explain her lack of experience. Instead she talks about the skills she has (and would have given more details if she hadn't discussed them earlier) and expresses her willingness to learn new ones.

Never Say: "I don't have a lot of experience, but how can I get any if no one will hire me?" Although what she is saying is true, this answer highlights the candidate's inexperience instead of addressing her attributes and willingness to learn.

Q You've worked at the same company since you graduated from high school fifteen years ago. Why are you looking for a new job now?

A I learned a lot at my current job and I was given the opportunity to take on many different responsibilities. I decided to get some formal training to enhance my skills in bookkeeping and word processing. That training qualifies me for a job that requires greater skills than my current one does.

This candidate wants to use his new skills and therefore must change jobs. This is reasonable and shows he is motivated to do the best he can.

Never Say: "I'm bored." Many people leave their jobs because they are bored. However, that's not a good way to impress a prospective employer. The candidate should name something specific about this new job that he is looking forward to.

Q You're so young. What makes you think you can do a good job?

A I have a lot of experience in retail. I started working as a retail clerk straight out of high school and over the last three years I worked my way up to assistant manager.

Rather than letting the interviewer lead her into a discussion about her age, this candidate leads him into a discussion about her experience.

Never Say: "What does my age have to do with it?" While it is reasonable to have reservations about the interviewer's motives, her approach is too confrontational.

Q Your resume doesn't show any formal training in this field. What do you think qualifies you for this job?

A While I don't have formal training in this field, I do have a lot of practical experience. As you can see from my resume, I spent a tremendous amount of time doing research in my last job. I plan to begin taking some courses so I can get my degree in this field.

This interviewee explains how her experience has given her the skills she needs to do this job. She also talks about her intention to get some formal training.

Never Say: "I'm going to get my degree." While this answer shows this candidate plans to develop her skills, it doesn't indicate she currently has the skills necessary for this job.

Q I see that all of your work experience has been in sales. What qualifies you to work in fundraising?

A Both sales and fundraising involve persuasion. In sales I had to persuade people to buy our products. I was very good at it. I had the highest level of sales of anyone in my division. Now I would like to use those skills to convince people to donate money to this organization.

This candidate discusses how he can transfer his sales skills to a career in fundraising.

Never Say: "I think I will really like this field a lot more." This doesn't adequately explain why he is qualified for the job.

Q I noticed your three previous jobs were in three different cities. Why did you move around so much?

A My wife was in the Marines, but she is retired now and working as a civilian in this city, so we're finally done moving around.

As a general rule, marital status should not be discussed on a job interview. However, the candidate must explain why he has moved around so much in the past and why he won't be doing that in the future.

Never Say: "I won't be moving around a lot anymore." The interviewee should give a more elaborate answer than this one. If he doesn't want to bring up his marital status, he can say there were reasons he had to move around in the past, but some changes have brought more stability to his life.

Q I see you were manager at Wanda's Whispers. What type of business is that and what did you do there?

A Wanda's Whispers is a retail store that sells women's lingerie. I was the store manager. I interviewed, hired, and trained the store's sales team.

Although she may be embarrassed to discuss the nature of the business, she proudly discusses her responsibilities there.

Never Say: "The store sells ladies' apparel." The candidate is so flustered when she has to discuss this job that she neglects to discuss what she did there.

 **Alert**

> You may be embarrassed by the nature of a company you worked for in the past. You don't have to go into details, but remember the employer can do his own research. Focus instead on what your duties were when you worked there and how they relate to the job for which you are applying.

Q You've been out of the workforce for five years. Why re-enter it now?

A I have a lot to offer. I've developed many skills over the last five years and I want to put them to use. I have excellent organization and time management skills. I am also great at resolving conflicts.

Rather than discuss how re-entering the workforce will benefit her, this candidate instead highlights what she can bring to the job.

Never Say: "I'm in the process of getting divorced, so I have to go back to work." This is more information than the candidate should share.

Q I see you have a GED. Why did you drop out of high school?

A I guess I was young and foolish then. It was a long time ago. I thought I didn't need school anymore, but I was sadly mistaken. I got my GED three years later and then went on to college. I'm looking forward to applying my training as a registered nurse to this position.

Youthful indiscretions can be forgiven. Although this candidate dropped out of high school, he did continue his education and is planning to move forward with his career.

Never Say: "I don't remember. It was a long time ago." That isn't something one would easily forget. Since the candidate has gone on to complete his education, he shouldn't be ashamed to talk about his past.

Q You didn't start working until two years after you got your degree. What were you doing?

A I traveled extensively the year after I graduated from college. I backpacked across Europe for three months and then I spent four months in Australia. After that I traveled across the United States.

Had this candidate said that she sat at home watching television for a year after graduating, the interviewer would have assumed she was a little low on motivation. However, she explored the world, which was an admirable use of her time.

Never Say: "I needed to take some time off. College was hard." Even if this candidate didn't have as interesting a story to tell as the previous candidate, she should have explained what she did during that time.

Q You've been working outside the banking industry for the last year. Can you explain why you want to return now?

A Yes, I can. The job market, as you know, has been bad for the last year and a half. It's been impossible for someone with my qualifications to find a job in the banking industry. In order to support my family, I had to take jobs in retail sales. I was happy to see your ad for a banking job that needs someone with my skills in branch management.

This candidate's only choice is to be honest. He is not to blame for the bad job market, so he makes no excuses for working outside his field for a year.

Never Say: "I wanted to try out a new industry." It's okay to try out a new industry, but this candidate should explain why he wants to return to his old one.

⚡ Alert

Employers often search the Internet for information about prospective employees. If there's anything inappropriate about you out there in cyberspace, remove it. If you are unsure about what might be considered inappropriate, think of things you wouldn't want your grandmother to see. Make your MySpace or Facebook page private if you have inappropriate content on it.

Q I did a little web search and found your MySpace page. That's some very interesting stuff you posted. Care to explain?

A Everyone has a work persona and a personal time persona, I think. You should know I take my job very seriously. That means I give it my full attention while I'm working.

This job hunter forgot to make her pages private. Since the interviewer has already found potentially embarrassing material about her online, she knows it's too late for denials. All she can do at this point is stress that her private life won't interfere with her work life.

Never Say: "What page?" or "What I do on my own time is my business." Playing dumb won't work if the evidence of your after-work behavior exists online. As for the second option, while you might feel your private time is yours to do with as you wish, you need to reassure a potential employer that your behavior won't spill over into your work life by, for example, making you late to work or causing you to arrive at work with a hangover.

Chapter 12

Dealing with Illegal Questions

EITHER OUT OF ignorance or blatant disregard for antidiscrimination laws, prospective employers sometimes ask questions that are often referred to as "illegal." Whether or not these questions are actually illegal will be discussed in this chapter. The employer usually doesn't have your best interests at heart if he asks them. If you know what your rights are before going into an interview, you will be able to recognize questions that are inappropriate, if not illegal.

Laws That Protect You from Discrimination

There are federal laws that make it illegal for employers to discriminate against employees and job applicants. These laws include Title VII of the Civil Rights Act of 1964, the Age Discrimination in Employment Act of 1967, and Title I of the Americans with Disabilities Act, all of which the Equal Employment Opportunity Commission (EEOC) oversees. The National Labor Relations Act, which is enforced by the National Labor Relations Board, is another law that protects individuals from job discrimination. The Civil Service Reform Act of 1978 prohibits federal agencies from discriminating against their workers and job applicants. Let's look at these laws and how they can protect you in more detail.

Title VII of the Civil Rights Act of 1964

Title VII of the Civil Rights Act of 1964 prohibits employers from discriminating against employees and prospective employees because of their race, color, religion, sex, or national origin.

RACE AND COLOR DISCRIMINATION

An employer cannot reject a job candidate based on the candidate's race or color. If an interviewer requests information that will disclose the candidate's race, the EEOC interprets it to mean the information obtained will be used as a basis for making a hiring decision. The request for that information would likely be used as evidence should the candidate bring charges of discrimination against the employer.

⌣Ě⌣ Alert

An employer can ask for information on race if it is needed for affirmative action purposes, in which case it would have to be kept separately from the information that is used to make a hiring decision.

NATIONAL ORIGIN DISCRIMINATION

An employer cannot discriminate against an individual because of her national origin, meaning the country she or her parents are from. Therefore, an interviewer may not ask you where you were born or where your parents were born. He may not ask you if you speak a foreign language unless it pertains to the duties of the job for which you are interviewing.

RELIGIOUS DISCRIMINATION

An employer cannot use an applicant's religious beliefs in deciding whether or not to hire you. An employer cannot ask you what your religion is, if you belong to any religious groups, or if you go to a house of worship. She also cannot ask if your religious beliefs prevent you from working on certain days.

PREGNANCY DISCRIMINATION

The Pregnancy Discrimination Act was passed in 1978 as an Amendment to Title VII of the Civil Rights Act. It states that as long as a woman is able to perform the major functions of her job, she cannot be passed over for employment because of a pregnancy-related condition. An interviewer cannot ask if you are pregnant or if you plan to become pregnant in the future.

 Fact

> State and municipal laws protect against job discrimination. They often take precedence over the federal laws. Some of these laws protect workers and job candidates against discrimination on the bases of sexual orientation, marital status, political affiliation, and parental status. Your local district office of the EEOC can help you determine if a prospective employer has broken a state or local law.

The Age Discrimination in Employment Act of 1967

The Age Discrimination in Employment Act makes it illegal for employers to discriminate against employees or job candidates on the basis of age. It protects those who are at least forty years old. An interviewer may not ask you how old you are or when you graduated from high school or college, since providing that information would force you to reveal your age.

Title I of the Americans with Disabilities Act of 1990

Title I of the Americans with Disabilities Act prohibits employers from discriminating against workers or job applicants who have disabilities. This law actually makes asking some questions illegal. The ADA prohibits an employer who has not yet made a job offer to a candidate from asking questions that are likely to reveal a candidate's disability. For example, an interviewer can't ask questions about health problems, such as a heart condition or asthma, or about mental illness. He cannot ask a candidate if she has a disability that would keep her from performing the job. Even if a candidate has an obvious disability or reveals a hidden one, the employer cannot ask about it. There is one exception. An employer can ask a job candidate to explain how she will perform specific job functions.

An employer may not require a candidate to take a medical exam prior to receiving a job offer. However, once the employer makes a job offer, he can make it contingent on the employee passing a medical exam, as long as the same is required of all candidates to whom the employer offers jobs in the same category. If the results of that exam reveal a disability, a job offer may be rescinded only if the employer's reason for doing so is "job-related and consistent with business necessity," according to the EEOC.

 **Question**

Is everyone protected by antidiscrimination laws?
Not all companies must adhere to federal discrimination laws. You can determine whether or not a company is required to follow a particular law by finding out how many workers it employs. This number varies by law but generally falls into a range of between fifteen and twenty employees.

National Labor Relations Act

The National Labor Relations Act regulates the way in which unions and private-sector employers interact. It gives employees the right to organize unions and to engage in union activities without interference from their employers. According to the National Labor

Relations Board, which administers the NLRA, an employer can't discriminate against a job candidate or employee because of her union affiliation.

Civil Service Reform Act

The Civil Service Reform Act of 1978 prohibits federal agencies from discriminating against job applicants and employees on the bases of race, color, national origin, religion, sex, age, disability, marital status, political affiliation, or sexual orientation. The U.S. Office of Special Council investigates reports of discrimination against federal job applicants.

What Questions Are Illegal?

Although we often hear people talk about illegal interview questions, most discrimination laws don't prohibit any questions outright. The exception is the ADA, which actually does say it is illegal to ask a job candidate whether she has a disability.

E ssential

If you believe an employer has discriminated against you, you can file a charge of discrimination with the EEOC. Call the EEOC at 1-800-669-4000 or 1-800-669-6820 (TTY) between 8:30 A.M. and 5:30 P.M. Eastern Standard Time to find out how to do this. You can also send an e-mail to *info@eeoc.gov*. In addition, instructions are available on the EEOC website, *www.eeoc.gov*.

As far as the other laws are concerned, the asking of the question itself is usually not illegal. It is problematic; it can demonstrate the employer's intent to discriminate. If an employer uses your answer to one of these questions to deny you a job, that can be considered discriminatory.

If you envision an interviewer being carted off to the police station in handcuffs after asking you an inappropriate question, you will be disappointed to learn that is an unlikely scenario. Even if the questions were illegal or information obtained during an interview was in fact used to discriminate against you, the job candidate would have to report the employer to the EEOC before any action would be taken. The result would be a lawsuit and possible fine, not jail time.

As a job applicant, you may be asked some sensitive questions. The next section deals with the right and wrong ways to handle them.

Questions and Answers

Q How old are you?

A I prefer to think of myself in terms of experience and not age. I have worked in this industry for quite some time. I have seen it go from a small playing field to what it is today. Fortunately, I have kept up with all the changes by taking classes and constantly updating my skills.

Rather than address the issue of age or the inappropriateness of this question, this candidate has instead decided to address some positive things about himself. He has a lot of experience and he strives to keep himself abreast of changes in the industry by taking classes.

Never Say: "I'm fifty-two, but I look young for my age." This applicant should have avoided revealing his age.

Q How much do you weigh?

A My weight isn't an issue. I have never had a problem performing my job duties.

This question is not only rude, it may be illegal as well, according to the ADA. This candidate explains how her weight doesn't affect her ability to do her job.

Never Say: "I'm thinking of getting my stomach stapled." Although he has asked a rude and possibly illegal question, the employer has learned that this candidate might need some time off from work, and she hasn't even started yet.

Q What is your race?

A I'm African American and Asian.

If an employer asks a question about race, her intentions are usually not good, so make a mental note that you were asked. If the employer discriminates against you based on your race, the information you provided in this answer can be used as evidence against her if you file a complaint with the EEOC.

Never Say: "That is an illegal question. You can't ask me that." You are certainly within your rights to take an interviewer to task for asking such an inappropriate question, but the question in itself isn't illegal unless the information garnered from it is used to discriminate against you.

Q Were you born in the United States?

A I'm not sure why you're asking me that. Can you explain?

This question is inappropriate and the employer probably knows that. The candidate gives him a chance to correct himself. Perhaps the employer needs to know if the candidate is eligible to work in the United States.

Never Say: "I came here from Poland two years ago." The candidate is not required to reveal that information.

Q Where were your parents born?

A My parents came to this country thirty years ago. They worked very hard to put me through school and are very proud of my successful career. They passed their work ethic down to me.

This candidate chooses not to reveal her national origin and instead manages to talk about her own qualities. There is nothing that says a candidate shouldn't reveal her national origin, only that she doesn't have to.

Never Say: "My parents are from Greece and Portugal." This candidate is giving out more information than is necessary.

☀ Alert

You should always make a point of sounding confident when answering questions on a job interview. If you sound unsure of yourself, the interviewer will pick up on it. Your confidence—or lack thereof—is also apparent in your body language, so be aware of what your posture and gestures say about you.

Q Your last name sounds Spanish. Is it?

A Yes, it is.

The applicant has a choice to make. He can refuse to answer or he can just give a simple answer, as he did. If this was the only question of this type, the interviewer may have just been trying to make conversation.

Never Say: "My father was born in Guatemala. My mother was born in Ireland." This candidate reveals more about his national origin than he needs to.

Q What is your sexual orientation?

A I don't think that has anything to do with this job.

Sexual orientation isn't something that should be discussed on a job interview.

Never Say: "I'm gay" or "I'm straight." While employers might, according to some state laws, be prohibited from using the answer to this question to discriminate against a job candidate because of her sexual orientation, this information isn't relevant to the job interview.

 Fact

There currently aren't any federal laws that protect private sector employees and job applicants from discrimination based on one's sexual orientation or gender identity. Some states and local municipalities have such laws, and the Civil Service Reform Act protects federal workers from discrimination based on sexual orientation.

Q How tall are you?

A I'm five foot seven.

Although an employer shouldn't ask an applicant about any physical characteristics, including height and weight, answering it shouldn't cause a problem.

Never Say: "You can't ask me that." While that is true, that response may unnecessarily cause hard feelings, especially if the interviewer meant no harm in asking it.

Q What is your religious background?

A I consider religion a very personal thing, so I would rather not discuss it.

The applicant can always choose to politely refuse to answer a question he considers improper. That is what he has decided to do.

Never Say: "How dare you ask me that?" While the candidate can refuse to answer the question, there is no reason to be that confrontational. That can certainly hurt your chances of getting hired.

Q Will your religion keep you from working on Saturday or Sunday?

A Perhaps we can discuss the details of my schedule after we both confirm that I'm the right candidate for this position.

This candidate knows Title VII of the Civil Rights Act requires that an employer reasonably accommodate the religious practices of an employee or applicant as long as doing so doesn't pose a hardship. She also knows that an employer cannot decide to reject a candidate based on the knowledge that this accommodation will be necessary. However, she chooses to wait until she receives an offer before discussing this.

Never Say: "I can't work on Saturday." Although the employer can't make a decision based on this information, it isn't necessary to discuss it at this point.

Q Do you have any children?

A I understand that you may be concerned that having a family might get in the way of someone's career. However, that has never been the case with me. I'm very dedicated to my career.

Without giving a direct answer to this question, the candidate has chosen to reassure the employer that having a family, or not having one, will not influence his career.

Never Say: "I don't have children yet." If the employer chooses not to hire this candidate, it may be because this answer indicates he might have children in the future. Whether or not this constitutes discrimination is debatable since he doesn't currently have children.

Essential

When faced with an improper question about your family or marital status, you can choose to address the issue head-on. You can reassure the interviewer that having a family has not and will not interfere with your career.

Q Are you planning to have children?

A I am very committed to my career. Whether or not I have children will not affect that.

This interviewee tells the employer the only thing she has the right to know—that she is dedicated to her career.

Never Say: "I've always wanted to have children." The candidate did not have to answer this question.

Q What child care arrangements do you have in place?

A I'm sensing that you may have concerns about scheduling. I have a great attendance record on my current job. I haven't missed a day of work in two years.

This candidate has decided to address the intent of the interviewer's question. Since he believes she is afraid that child care problems will cause him to miss work, he informs her of his perfect attendance record.

Never Say: "My child goes to day care." The employer is out of line in asking this question. However, this candidate's answer only heightens her concern since a child will not be able to go to day care when he is ill. That means Mom or Dad may have to miss work.

Q Are you married?

A No, I'm not.

Although this question is inappropriate and may even be illegal depending on state or municipal laws, the candidate sees no harm in answering it.

Never Say: "I'm getting married in six months and let's see . . . sixteen days." This answer implies that the interviewee is very immersed in her wedding plans and perhaps may not be able to give the necessary attention to her job.

Q Do you belong to a union?

A Will I be required to join a union?

The NLRA prohibits employers from questioning applicants about their union sympathies. This candidate chooses to avoid the question by asking his own.

Never Say: "Yes." The employer can't make a decision based on this information and shouldn't have asked it in the first place. The candidate certainly didn't have to answer it.

Q Are you a Democrat or Republican?

A I've always felt that it's a bad idea to discuss politics with any-one. Therefore, I'm going to refrain from answering that question.

The candidate has given a polite answer but has refused to pro-vide the information the interviewer improperly requested.

Never Say: "I'm a Democrat." Your political affiliation has noth-ing to do with how well you perform on the job. There is no reason an interviewer needs to know this.

 Fact

There aren't any federal laws that protect private sector employ-ees or job applicants from discrimination on the basis of political affiliation. The Civil Service Reform Act prohibits federal govern-ment agencies from discriminating against employees or job can-didates because of their political affiliation. Some state and local laws also make this type of discrimination illegal.

Q Will your spouse mind the long hours you will have to work here?

A I've always worked very long hours so this won't be a problem.

This candidate chooses to address the question about the long hours she will be required to work rather than address her marital status.

Never Say: "My husband would love me to get a job with fewer hours, but there aren't many like that out there." There is no reason to give this much information. The interviewee's answer will set off some alarms. Since her husband is unhappy with her hours, she would probably take a job with fewer hours if it came along.

Q How do you want to be addressed? Miss or Mrs.?

A You can just call me Robin.

The interviewer is trying to ascertain the candidate's marital status, but she won't play into it. She dodges the issue altogether.

Never Say: "I prefer Mrs. Brown." The candidate could have avoided letting the interviewer know her marital status.

Essential

When an interviewer asks you an improper question, you have three basic options. You can refuse to answer it, you can confront the interviewer, or you can answer it. Information you give voluntarily can be used against the employer if he discriminates.

Q Have you ever been arrested or convicted of a crime?

A No. I have never been convicted of a crime.

According to the law in many states, an employer may not ask you if you have ever been arrested, but, depending on where the employer is located, he may be able to ask you if you've been convicted of a crime. In some states convictions for certain types of crimes can be used when considering whether to hire a job candidate. Notice how this candidate avoids the arrest question. She doesn't want to lie or discuss an arrest that she was not convicted for.

Never Say: "I was arrested once but I wasn't convicted." Again, depending on the law in your state, the employer may only ask about prior convictions. The applicant may not have to talk about her arrest at all.

Q Have you ever committed a crime?

A If you're asking if I've ever been convicted of a crime, no I haven't been.

If the employer is located in a state that prohibits discrimination based on a candidate's arrest record, but allows hiring decisions to be made based on whether or not someone has been convicted, the applicant is not required to reveal prior arrests or criminal behavior.

Never Say: "Yes, but I was never convicted."

 **Question**

What should I do if I was in jail?
If you were convicted of a felony, this information will be revealed in a background check. You might as well be up front about it. If the prospective employer is located in a state that only allows a conviction to weigh into a hiring decision if it is for a crime directly related to the job description, then the law may protect you from discrimination.

Q I see you're limping. Did you hurt yourself?

A I'm fine, thank you.

The employer, according to the ADA, cannot inquire about an applicant's injury and the candidate is under no obligation to reveal it.

Never Say: "I have cerebral palsy." The candidate is not required to reveal any information regarding his disability.

Q Do you have a heart condition?

A With all due respect, I don't have to answer that question.

The applicant has a right to refuse to answer this question. The ADA makes it illegal for an employer to ask questions about a job candidate's health.

Never Say: "Yes, I do." The employer is legally prohibited from asking this question and the candidate does not have to answer it.

 Fact

The ADA prohibits an employer from asking about the nature of an applicant's disability. It does allow an employer to inquire about a candidate's ability to perform a job-related task and, in some cases, may even ask the applicant to demonstrate how she will perform that task.

Q Will you need us to make any accommodations in order for you to do your job?

A I am able to perform all functions of the job as you described it.

The ADA prohibits the employer from asking this question, even if he asks it of all applicants.

Never Say: "Yes, I will." The applicant doesn't have to answer this question. If she chooses to, the employer can't decide not to hire her because of her answer, unless the accommodations she needs will cause the employer undue hardship.

Q Have you ever been treated for mental health problems?

A I have, but everything is under control now. I have always performed well at work and I know I will continue to.

Although he is under no obligation to reveal this information at any time, this candidate doesn't want to lie to his employer and knows that the truth may come out at some point in the future.

Never Say: "No, I haven't" if you have. This candidate just lied to his prospective employer. Although he is within his legal rights to withhold information regarding his mental health, he has to consider whether he plans to reveal this information at a later date and what the consequences may be if he does. Although the employer can't fire an employee because of the employee's mental illness, she may distrust him for lying, which will damage their relationship. He would be better off telling the truth or simply saying he'd rather not discuss it.

 Fact

An employer can refuse to hire someone who currently uses illegal drugs. The ADA does not protect the applicant in this case. In addition, tests for illegal drugs are not subject to the ADA's restrictions on medical examinations.

Q Have you ever been treated for drug addiction?

A That was some time ago and I prefer not to discuss it.

This candidate is within his rights not to discuss this. Those who have been treated for drug addiction are covered by the ADA, and a hiring decision cannot be based upon this.

Never Say: "Yes, and I've only slipped up twice since then." The ADA doesn't protect someone who is currently using drugs from discrimination.

Q Do you currently take any prescription drugs?

A I've taken medication from time to time, but it has never affected my work.

The candidate doesn't have to answer this question but doesn't want to be dishonest. It's her call to make. This answer does not reveal whether the candidate is currently taking medication, and by law she doesn't have to reveal that.

Never Say: "Yes, I take pain medication." There is no reason the candidate needed to reveal such specific information.

Q Travel is a big part of this job. Will your family be okay with that?

A I can assure you that traveling will not be a problem. I traveled extensively on my previous job.

This candidate has chosen to let the employer know that his family status will not affect his job. He mentions the fact that his previous job had similar requirements and it wasn't a problem.

Never Say: "Traveling shouldn't be a problem. I just have to make sure my wife and I aren't out of town at the same time." By giving this answer, the candidate acknowledges that traveling could be a problem.

Q You're a young single woman living in the city. How do you handle having men chase after you?

A Work has always been my priority.

It is inappropriate for the employer to ask a question regarding the applicant's sex life. The candidate chooses to evade the question by talking about work.

Never Say: "Can you believe I'm dating five different men right now?" This candidate has chosen to answer a question she didn't have to and in doing so may cause the employer to wonder how she will have any time for work.

Essential

When discussing what you would do if you were hired, you should draw on your past experience. Talk about how you completed similar projects on your last job or how you made similar decisions.

Q Whom should we notify in case of an emergency?

A I have to give it some thought. Can I let you know?

The employer does not need this information before the employee begins to work for her. This may be a thinly disguised attempt to learn about the candidate's personal life; for example, his marital status.

Never Say: "You can notify my wife. Her name is . . ." This answer reveals more than the employer needs to know about the candidate's personal life.

Q Asked of a candidate applying for a job with the U.S. government: "Are you gay?"

A That isn't relevant to this job.

While a job candidate may or may not choose to answer this question, her answer can't play a role in a federal government agency's decision to hire her. Federal job applicants are protected from discrimination by the Civil Service Reform Act.

Never Say: "None of your business." Being confrontational is never the right way to go, even if you feel a question is inappropriate, rude, or even illegal. If you don't want to share this information, it is always best to be polite.

Q Do you want to have dinner on Saturday night? We can discuss your job qualifications over a nice bottle of pinot.

A I'll have to say no thank you. I never mix business with pleasure.

If the interviewer is persistent or in any way makes the candidate feel like he will get a job offer only by going out on a date with her, this may be considered sexual harassment, which is illegal under Title VII of the Civil Rights Act of 1964. It can be reported to the EEOC. The candidate makes it clear that the employer's advances are unwelcome, a necessary element to a sexual harassment claim.

Never Say: "What time on Saturday?" The job candidate should never acquiesce to this kind of advance.

Chapter 13

Behavioral Interviews

IN CHAPTERS 4 and 8 you learned how to answer questions about your skills and abilities. You were urged to give more than yes and no answers to questions of this sort. It is always wise to provide an example of when you used a particular attribute. Behavioral interviews take this concept of using real-life examples to demonstrate your attributes a few steps further. You will not only have the opportunity to talk about *when* you used a particular attribute, but also explain *how* you used it.

Behavioral Interviews: The Basics

Potential employers use behavioral interviews to help them determine how job candidates will react to certain situations based on how they responded in past experiences.

How Behavioral Interview Techniques Help Employers

When an employer conducts an interview, his main objective is to make sure the person he hires can do the job. The best way to find out whether someone can do a job is to actually watch him do it. Generally, though, a prospective employer has to assess several candidates for an open position, and time is usually of the essence when it comes to making a hiring decision. In most cases, it would be inefficient to evaluate job candidates by actually having them do the job for which they are interviewing. Furthermore, since many people are currently employed while they are engaged in a job search, it would be difficult to schedule these "auditions."

In lieu of actually trying out job candidates to determine which one is best for a particular job, what can an employer do? Many employers use a technique called behavioral interviewing, which relies on the theory that past behavior is a good predictor of future behavior. Specifically, this type of interview attempts to determine how the job candidate drew upon her competencies to handle situations on a previous job or jobs in order to predict how she will handle similar situations if this employer hires her.

🄴 Fact

During your job search, you may be faced with a behavioral interview, a standalone entity during which an interviewer asks you only behaviorally oriented questions. Alternately, behavioral questions may be incorporated into your regular interview, in which case only some of the questions an interviewer asks you will be behaviorally oriented.

What Happens During a Behavioral Interview?

Before an employer begins interviewing candidates, he will determine what knowledge, skills, and abilities are required for the job. Together these are referred to as competencies, and they may include the following:

- Decision-making skills
- Time management skills
- Problem-solving skills
- Organizational skills
- The ability to multitask

- Interpersonal skills
- Writing and presentation skills
- The ability to work on and build teams
- Flexibility

During a behavioral interview, the interviewer will ask you to demonstrate that you have the competencies needed to do the job. You will have to draw upon real-life examples that illustrate how you used a particular competency in a work-related situation.

How to Answer Behavioral Questions

When answering behavioral questions, you want to show the interviewer that you not only have a particular competency, but that you used it to benefit a past employer. Behavioral questions possibly require the most preparation of any you will be asked on a job interview.

Essential

Your research will help you figure out how to answer many of the behavioral questions the interviewer might ask you. Use your network to locate people who may have experience with that employer. The more you can find out about a company, the better you will understand the qualities it is looking for in an employee.

If you know what competencies the employer desires, it will be easier for you to prepare for the interview. To find out what competencies an employer requires, first turn to the job description. You may find them listed there; if you don't, you may have to dig a little deeper to learn what competencies an employer requires of a new hire.

Once you know what competencies the employer wants an employee to have, you need to come up with some anecdotes that highlight those competencies. Look to your work history—or your school experiences if you are a recent graduate—to find real-life situations in which you used your knowledge, skills, and abilities to successfully solve a problem or complete a project or task.

When you answer a behavioral question, first present the task or problem you faced. Then explain what steps you took to accomplish the task or solve the problem, making sure to highlight the competencies you used. The interviewer probably won't state what competency she expects you to demonstrate. You will have to quickly analyze the question to figure it out. Give as many details as necessary to best demonstrate each competency you determine she is looking for, but be careful not to go off on a tangent.

Questions and Answers

Q Tell me about something you've done to motivate your coworkers.

A About a year ago our company went through some tough times and about twenty-five workers were laid off. Morale was lower than I had ever seen it. This happened right around the time we had to start putting together our holiday issue, and no one was really into it. I planned a "winter in July" party to pick up everyone's spirits and to get us ready to work on the magazine. By the time the party was over, we were all in a better mood and we were ready to put together a great issue. I think it was one of the best ones we ever did.

The job candidate has demonstrated that he knows how to motivate others.

Q What is the toughest group you had to get to cooperate with you?

A I was asked to teach a new procedure to the customer service team. I had heard rumblings to the effect that many people on the team were unhappy with the new procedures, so I knew I wasn't going to have a receptive group to work with. Before I could be effective at teaching them what they needed to know, I had to convince them that the new procedure would benefit them. I set up a presentation that explained how it would save them time. Once the team saw the benefits of the new procedure, they actually looked forward to the training. They learned very quickly and we were able to implement the procedure in less than a week.

The interviewee demonstrates two competencies in her response. She highlights her interpersonal skills when she talks about how she was aware of the customer service team's concerns. Then she highlights her presentation skills.

Q Describe a situation in which you had a positive influence on someone else's actions.

A One of the new guys in my department was assigned a couple of projects at once and couldn't figure out how he would get both of them done on time. He was really frantic since he had only been there for a short time and was approaching his first performance evaluation. He knew only too well that these projects were crucial to his getting a good evaluation. When he told me about his concerns, I asked him how he was scheduling his work and whether he was setting deadlines for completing different portions of his project. He had no idea what I was talking about. This was his first real job and it required a different sort of time management than his college courses had. I spent a lunch hour teaching him how to set up work schedules. After we met he set up work schedules for both projects and asked me to look them over. I did and helped him make a couple of changes. He completed both projects by their deadlines and got a pretty good performance evaluation.

In describing how she helped her colleague, this candidate shows that she has good interpersonal skills. She also manages to demonstrate her own time management skills by describing how she taught her coworker to set a schedule for himself.

Fact

In today's workplace, most people work on teams. A team must function as a single entity whose goal it is to complete a project efficiently and effectively. Members of teams must appreciate one another's differences and be willing to compromise. You must be able to demonstrate that you can work well as part of a team.

Q We expect the person we hire for this job to be able to take charge of a couple of big projects. Are you ready for that?

A A few months ago the chairperson of my department asked me to assemble a committee, made up of faculty and students, to evaluate the current curriculum. He gave us two semesters to complete the project. The first thing I had to do was decide who to include on the committee. I chose a few members of the faculty who had been with us for a very long time, as well as some who had recently joined the department. The students I picked ranged from freshmen to graduate students. I wanted a wide cross-section of both faculty and students. After that I set up deadlines for certain parts of the project to be completed and I set up a schedule for meetings. Finally, each person was assigned a specific area to look at and then present for discussion at each meeting. Based on the work of this committee, we were able to drop some courses that were not effectively meeting the goals of the department. We were able to add innovative courses that would attract students.

By giving this answer, the candidate demonstrates that she is good at organizing and planning projects.

 **Question**

What should I do if I can't use a real-life experience to demonstrate a competency?
If you can't draw upon real-life experience to answer a question, don't make something up. You can use a hypothetical situation as an example, but let the interviewer know you are doing that.

Q Have you ever been a member of a group where some of the members did not work well together? Describe what you did.

A Yes, I have. I was a member of a group that was developing a new software program for kids. There were three of us on the team. I got along with the two people I was working with, but they didn't get along with each other at all. They constantly shot down each other's ideas and they expected me to take sides. I refused to do that. Instead I tried to help them see each other's point of view. I explained how they each had good ideas and helped them compromise. In the end we had a very successful product.

With this answer, the job candidate demonstrates that he has good interpersonal skills and good team-building skills.

Q Give an example of a time when you went above and beyond the call of duty.

A I've been teaching algebra for seven years and I know some children really have difficulty understanding it. There's only so much individual attention I can give to each student during class, so any help I give them has to be at another time. I teach five classes a day, which leaves only two free periods. One is a prep period and one is my lunchtime. I decided the kids needed math help more than I needed lunch, so I set aside three times a week when they could come to my room for tutoring. Many students have taken me up on this extra help and their grades have improved significantly. Most of my students do really well on the statewide seventh-grade test as a result of my tutoring them.

This candidate demonstrates how she solved a problem within the time constraints of her job. She shows how her students and the school benefited.

Q Have you ever been assigned several project at the same time? How did you handle it?

A That happens very often, but one time that stands out in my mind is last year during the fall. The managers of three departments—women's outerwear, toys, and women's accessories—asked me to set up their winter holiday displays. They all wanted them up within a week. I knew there was no way I could complete all three in one week. Since I know customers are more likely to shop for kids' presents first and kids really enjoy the displays, I decided to decorate the toy department first. I checked with the other two managers to see if they had some flexibility in their scheduling and both did. I scheduled both departments to have their displays up the following week. All three departments were beautifully decorated for the holidays and I completed them all in two weeks.

This interviewee demonstrates knowledge about his industry when he discusses why he chose to decorate the toy department first. He goes on to show how he is good at planning and scheduling.

Q Can you give an example of how you adjust to unforeseen circumstances?

A Last summer I was less than a week away from a big presentation. I was in the middle of preparing for it when all of a sudden the power went out. We soon found out the lights were out everywhere on the East Coast and there were no estimates of how long that would be the case. Fortunately I was two days ahead of schedule in my preparation, but since I didn't know when power would be restored I was worried I wouldn't be able to work on my presentation. I knew if I wasn't ready on time, my company would look bad and it could cost us a lot of money. Our battery backup was still working, so I decided to print out the presentation. I wrote a lot of the presentation by hand that day. All I had left to do were my slides, which I did when the power came back on the next afternoon.

The job candidate shows that he knows how to cope with an emergency.

Q Give an example of a quick decision you made.

A When we were working on our April issue last year, one of the designers we planned to feature backed out just before the photo shoot because she didn't feel her line was ready. We had planned to feature her work on about twenty pages. Now we had to figure out what to do with those pages. We didn't have much time to waste. The photographer was on his way and was going to get paid for a day's work whether we used him or not. It turned out one of my assistant editors knew an up-and-coming designer. I decided to take a chance on the new designer since I trusted my assistant's opinion. The shoot was wonderful and her designs were fantastic. The issue was great and we've featured that designer a few times since then.

This interviewee shows that she knows how to make quick decisions.

Q This is a busy office and we have a lot of projects going on at once. Everyone who works here must be able to multitask. Can you?

A Since I work for three lawyers, I regularly have to multitask. Just two weeks ago they walked into my office one after another, handed me files, and told me they needed the work in them completed by the end of the week. I looked at the files and I figured out how long each assignment would take. Then I looked to see if there was any overlap between the assignments. I discovered that each required some research, which I was able to do that afternoon. The next morning I began working on the first project. I needed some additional files to do the other two projects, so I asked one of the file clerks to retrieve those for me while I put the finishing touches on the first assignment. With those files in front of me, I was able to work on the other two assignments.

While explaining his ability to multitask, this candidate also highlights his project-planning skills and his ability to delegate some work to others.

Q Give me an example of when you showed initiative and took the lead on a project.

A A year ago we noticed that our students' grades on statewide language arts exams were slipping. I had recently attended a seminar that addressed this particular issue and ways to resolve it. I had a program in mind that I thought we could implement at our school. I spoke to my principal about it and she asked me to write a formal proposal. After I did that and she approved it, I put together a committee of teachers and parents who would work with me to implement the program. This year's exam, as you know, won't take place until next month, but I think we'll see big improvements.

By giving this answer, the candidate shows how he recognized a problem and took initiative in resolving it.

Q Tell me about a report you had to write.

A My boss asked me to develop a plan to improve our quality-control process. She gave me a month to come up with three different ideas and said she would choose the best one based on my report. The first thing I noticed was that we didn't have a written document that described the procedure we were currently using, so I had to put one together. Then I began to research quality-control processes used by other companies. The librarian at our local library was able to tell me what databases I could access to find articles that discussed this issue. Through my research I was able to find which quality-control processes were most successful. I chose the three that I thought would work best for my employer and wrote about them. The report included my recommendation as to which one I thought we should use. My boss was pleased with the report. She agreed with my recommendation and my next project involved implementing the new process, including writing a document that described it completely.

This answer demonstrates this candidate's ability to put together a written report, including using research skills.

Essential

Certain soft skills are vital to one's performance at work. Without these skills, the employee simply can't do his job. Make a point of demonstrating that you have these valuable skills, even if you aren't specifically asked about them. They include multitasking, organizing, time management, and decision-making.

Q Give me an example of how you dealt with a conflict between two of your employees.

A A year ago two of my employees started having problems getting along with each other. It came from out of the blue but looked like it had the potential to escalate rapidly. I called separate meetings with each of the employees. They had remarkably similar stories and they didn't blame each other for their hard feelings. They agreed on a joint meeting, where I was able to help them realize that they really were on the same page after all. Things between them are now back to the way they were. They are both productive members of my department, so I'm glad we were able to work things out.

This candidate demonstrates her skill in conflict resolution.

Q Describe a recent unpopular decision you made and what the result was.

A A few months ago we found that we were having difficulty scheduling people to cover the circulation desk during lunch hours. Almost everyone wanted to go to lunch at 1 P.M., which meant we wouldn't have enough people around to check books in and out for our patrons. I decided that the only way to deal with this was to schedule lunch hours. We had two lunch hours—noon to 1 P.M. and 1 P.M. to 2 P.M. Staff could go to lunch only at the time they were assigned. No one liked this idea very much because they were used to going to lunch whenever they felt like it. Something had to be done, however, because if we didn't do something service would suffer. Scheduled lunch hours have been in effect for the past three months. The staff have gotten used to it and service has definitely improved.

The interviewer shows he is a good manager who isn't afraid to make decisions that may be unpopular.

Q Have you ever had to work with someone with whom you had a bad relationship? How did you handle it?

A My boss asked me to work on a project with the one person in my company I don't get along with. I knew we'd be working together for several months, and I didn't want those months to be miserable.

I decided to swallow my pride and invite my coworker to lunch. We discussed the project and what we would have to do to make it work. We both realized that the company would be the victim if we let our personal differences get in the way of our performance. We divided the project up so that we could each work independently using our individual strengths, but we wound up working together more than we expected, so we learned to appreciate each other's strengths and how to use them in combination to benefit the company. We completed the project and we've worked on several other ones together since then by choice. Even though we still don't always agree on things, we know how to work well together now.

The candidate demonstrates how she used her interpersonal skills to resolve her differences with her coworker.

 Fact

When an employer hires someone, he is investing in that person's future at his company. The more successful that person is and the longer she stays, the bigger the return on the investment. If he makes a poor hiring decision, that investment won't pay off because the person won't succeed and won't stick around. That is one reason employers take job interviewing very seriously.

Q Tell me about a recent situation in which you had to deal with a very upset customer.

A Just last week one of our customers called and was extremely upset because something we had shipped to him arrived damaged. One of his customers was coming in to pick up the item two days later and he didn't want to disappoint her. I assured him that he would have the item for his customer on time. I brought the merchandise to the shipping department myself and asked that it be sent out by overnight delivery. He called the next day to say his package had arrived. He thanked us for resolving this quickly and placed another order.

The candidate has demonstrated how his good interpersonal skills kept a customer happy and resulted in another sale.

Q Tell me about the most difficult person you've ever had to work with.

A That would have to be Jen. Jen was a perfectly nice person but she liked giving her work to others. She didn't have the right to do that. Our supervisor was the one who assigned work to us and he expected each of us to handle that work on our own. One day I decided I had had enough of this. Jen asked me to make some phone calls for her, and I told her we needed to have a talk. We did, and it turned out that Jen was overwhelmed by all the work our boss assigned and she didn't know how to handle it, other than by getting help from her coworkers. I helped her figure out a way to manage her time better and get her work done on her own. Jen is doing a lot better now. She doesn't try to pass off her work to other people anymore.

This candidate shows he has good interpersonal skills and is willing to help others succeed.

Q Describe a situation in which you were able to effectively "read" another person and guide your actions based on what you understood about her needs and values.

A About eight months ago, a client approached us about a new product they were introducing. There were two people I could have assigned to work on that project. Both would have done a good job; they are equally skilled and had worked with the client before. Knowing what I know about one of those employees, I had a feeling this new product was contrary to some of his personal values. I didn't want to jump to any conclusions, so I spoke to him before I made a decision about this. I was correct. He would have worked on the project, but he wouldn't have been comfortable with it. I decided to assign it to the other person. The client was very happy with the way things went. The product was introduced over the summer and has been very successful. They've had sales of about $1.5 million.

This candidate demonstrates her interpersonal skills by giving this answer.

Essential

Your impulsive nature may be admired by your friends but it may not be admired by a prospective employer. Your boss expects you to think through all your decisions carefully. Your response to questions on your interview should in no way reveal that you are impulsive.

Q Have you ever anticipated a problem while working on a project and found a way to avoid it?

A While working on a project in October, I realized the person who had done the budget hadn't included printing costs. It wasn't going to be a huge expense, but it was definitely something that needed to be included in the budget. First I figured out what the cost of printing would be. Then I looked at the rest of the budget to see if the other costs on it were accurate. I found a few places where the costs had been overstated a little bit. I was able to change some numbers around so the money allotted for those expenses could instead be used for printing. We were still a little short, so I had to talk to my boss about increasing the budget. He was able to do that because the amount we needed wasn't very significant.

Not only does this candidate demonstrate that she can anticipate and avoid problems, she also shows that she knows how to budget expenses.

☀ Alert

Your goals should always be aligned with those of the employer. If the employer senses that your goals have nothing to do with your prospective job, you probably won't be working for him anytime soon. Goals like cutting costs and increasing productivity are always appreciated. Reaching your own goals will be a by-product of that.

Q Have you ever found working on a team disappointing? Did you do anything that helped things improve?

A In a business course I took in college, we were assigned to teams to work on a project that involved running a mock company. At the beginning we had trouble working together. However, we were being graded as a group, so we had to find a way to utilize our differences rather than let them defeat us. I thought the project would be more successful if we drew on every member's strengths and interests. Once I explained this to everyone, we once again divided up the tasks, using our different strengths and interests to put together a successful project. We ended up earning an A.

The interviewee takes this opportunity to demonstrate her team-building skills as well as her leadership skills.

Q Tell me about a problem you solved.

A I was coordinating a trade show in Washington, D.C. We advertised in all the industry publications and got an unprecedented number of responses from vendors who wanted to display their products. There were 350 companies that wanted to reserve booths. I knew our current venue had insufficient space. We could have turned away some of the vendors, but since they represented a significant amount of revenue, I didn't think this was even an option. I started looking into larger venues. I thought the Washington Convention Center would be perfect. There was plenty of room to accommodate everyone, and with the extra participation we were able to afford the larger site. We went ahead and booked it. The trade show was very successful. Both attendees and vendors were thrilled with the event. Many expressed an interest in attending next year.

The interviewee demonstrates his problem-solving skills.

Q Tell me about a time when you had to use your presentation skills to influence a client.

A My former employer had one particular client who had to be convinced that our way was the best way to go every time we made a presentation. She always needed a lot of reassurance, which was her right since she was paying good money for our services. There was one particular project I worked on for her where she needed even more convincing than usual. She wanted to redesign the packaging for one of her hair-care products. We put together a package design that was unique; the bottle was oval shaped instead of the usual cylindrical shape. It would really stand out from everything else on the shelves. Since it was an unconventional design and she was pretty conservative, she was hesitant to proceed. I asked our research department to put together some focus groups. Ninety percent of those we surveyed said they liked the new design better than the old one, and 85 percent picked that product from a group of three other similar products. We presented that information to the client and sold her on the oval shape. She went ahead with it and saw a 22 percent increase in sales in the first six months after the new design was introduced.

This interviewee demonstrates his presentation skills as he is asked to and shows how he was able to influence his client's decision.

Fact

Always use actual figures to prove your point. If you are talking about increasing sales, raising money, or cutting costs, for example, give the actual dollar amount or the percentage of increase or decrease. For example, say that you increased sales by 20 percent or cut costs by $300,000.

Q Tell me how you delegate work effectively.

A One of our clients asked us to work on a major project for them. It involved a conference they were holding in six months. They expected thousands of people to attend and they needed us to help them choose a location, get the best rates on hotels, find caterers, and then organize the event. I picked three people on my staff to work on this project with me. One person had a lot of experience in travel, so I asked her to choose the location and work with some hotels in the area to get us the best rates for those who were attending the conference. Another person had worked on an event for a different client and he had done a great job choosing the caterer, so I asked him to arrange for the meals and refreshments. Finally, I picked the most organized person on my staff to collect responses from those who signed up for the conference. She had to assign them to tables for meals and had to figure out who would attend which conference events. I have to say my staff did a great job. I was so proud of them. More than 5,000 people attended the conference and all went well.

This candidate shows how he was able to delegate work to those who were most suitable for each assignment.

Q Give me an example of a time when you used your fact-finding skills to solve a problem.

A I was advisor to a student who needed to request a leave of absence from the university. I didn't know what the proper procedures were to officially do this. I didn't want to have her do it incorrectly and then be inadvertently dropped from the program. I asked our department secretary if there was a written document that discussed the procedure. He didn't know of one, so I contacted the registrar's office. They referred me to the associate dean's office. I finally got the answer there and was able to tell the student what she needed to do.

The candidate, as asked, demonstrates how she used her fact-finding skills.

 **Question**

> **Is it okay to make it seem as if I have experience I don't really have?**
> Never lie on a job interview. While having insufficient experience lowers your chances of getting hired, getting caught in a lie pretty much guarantees that you won't get the job. Instead of lying, talk about your related experience and explain how it is similar to what your prospective employer wants.

Q Tell me about a time when you had to make an unpopular decision.

A As director of our after-school program, I noticed that parents were often arriving very late to pick up their children. That meant that staff had to stay late too, which meant we had to pay them for their time. We simply didn't have the money to do that. I decided we would have to charge parents if they were late in order to have the money to pay our staff. Many people weren't happy with this, but we really didn't have a choice. This was enough incentive to get most parents to pick up their children on time. As a matter of fact, late pickups decreased by 85 percent right after this program went into effect.

This answer demonstrates that the candidate is willing to make an unpopular decision in order to solve a problem.

Q Tell me about a project you initiated.

A Last February, my boss took a three-week vacation. He left me some work to do while he was gone, but I finished it by the end of the first week. I had wanted to reorganize our files for a long time, and now I had the time to work on this. First I developed a plan to work on the project. I set up a schedule that included setting goals for what I wanted to complete by the end of each day in order to finish within two weeks. Then I figured out what filing system I wanted to use. I recruited our intern to help me. We finished the project on the Friday before my boss was set to return. He was happy to see what I had done while he was gone.

This answer demonstrates several competencies. The candidate takes initiative when she takes on a project without being asked. She shows that she knows how to plan and schedule a project and also how to delegate tasks.

Q Describe a big presentation you had to deliver.

A I had to make a big presentation at a national trade show. I was standing in for my supervisor who had to be somewhere else that day. He gave me the assignment two weeks before the show, so I had to prepare the presentation within a pretty tight time frame. First I set goals for completing each part of the presentation. Then I scheduled meetings with the developers of the products I'd have to present at the show so I could make sure I knew everything I could about them. I put together a great presentation. We took orders from 150 retailers that day alone and the sales on the products I presented increased by 15 percent after the show.

The candidate highlights her time management skills when she describes how she put together a presentation within a tight time frame. She also highlights her presentation skills. Notice that she backs up her answers by using real numbers.

Essential

When deciding which accomplishments to discuss on a job interview, you should always select those that best demonstrate your ability to do the job for which you are interviewing. For example, if you are interviewing for a job in an accounting firm and you've previously worked at one, use examples from that experience rather than from your experience at an advertising agency.

Q How have you convinced your boss that your approach is the best one to take in order to complete a project?

A Before I started working for my current employer, employees rarely worked in teams. I knew of many projects which a team could handle more effectively than an individual could, but I couldn't seem to convince anyone else. Then my boss's supervisor asked him to work on a huge project with a very tight deadline. Even though my supervisor is a talented man, this project clearly needed the talents of many different people to be successful. But I had to make him see that. I put together a list of people in different departments who had the necessary skills to help complete the project. I presented this list to my boss and sold him on the idea of putting together a team. He and his new team completed the project and his boss was extremely happy with it. My supervisor often uses teams to complete projects now.

This job candidate demonstrates how she was able to persuade her boss that her approach was the best one to take and goes as far as discussing the outcome of the project.

Q What you do when you have a conflict with a client?

A Last March I was working on a client's project that required us to hire a researcher. We worked closely with the client to draw up a contract with the researcher, who then completed the work. The client then decided he wanted some additional research done, but didn't want to pay for it. Of course, our researcher couldn't work for free, so we worked out a deal with her. We "loaned" her one of our interns to assist her, and she was able to charge less for the work she did. The client was happy that he got what he wanted and didn't have to pay full price for it. We were happy because he was pleased with our work, which meant that he would probably return in the future.

This interviewee shows how he resolves a conflict with a client by coming up with a solution with which everyone was happy.

Q Please tell me about a time you had to fire someone.

A One of my employees started coming into work late daily. When it first started happening, I called her into my office to find out what was going on. I thought she might have a personal problem that was keeping her from getting to work on time. She assured me that she would make sure to get there punctually. The lateness stopped, but it started again a month later. I called her to my office again and reminded her that tardiness was unacceptable. Our company was big on flex-time, so I offered her a later schedule. She turned it down, saying she couldn't work any later in the evening. Again she started arriving on time, but this time it only lasted two weeks. I had to let her go at that point. I explained the situation to her and she didn't seem very surprised.

This answer highlights the candidate's managerial skills.

Chapter 14

Do You Have Any Questions?

IF YOU LIKE talking about yourself, you'll sure get your fill of it when you go on job interviews. The majority of each one will revolve around you. The interviewer will spend a great deal of time asking you questions that will help him learn as much about you as he can. He will use what he learns to determine if he should hire you. When you have given him all the information he wants, the interviewer will finally offer you the chance to ask some questions of your own. He will learn almost as much from the questions you ask as he does from your answers to the ones he asks.

Asking Questions Is a Must

Never forgo the chance to ask a prospective employer questions. One important reason, perhaps the most important one, for asking questions at the conclusion of a job interview is that it helps you learn about the employer. The information you gather, in addition to the research you did before the interview, can help you decide whether you will want to consider a job offer from this employer. Let's say, though, you think you already know enough about this particular company to make a decision. You did a lot of research prior to the interview and, based on what you know, you'd accept a decent job offer. What would be the point of asking questions if you already have all the information you need? There are reasons for asking questions at the conclusion of a job interview that go beyond helping you decide whether you want to work for the company.

Why Ask Questions?

When you ask questions you indicate to the interviewer you are interested in the job. Since the company will probably want to avoid making an offer to a candidate who will reject it, not asking questions may take you out of the running for the job because it will make you look disinterested.

Your questions can either demonstrate to the interviewer that you were paying attention during the interview or they can show her you were not. Questions that follow up on points that were discussed during the interview are good. For example, if you need clarification on something, this would be a good time to ask for it. However, if you ask simple questions that she already answered at some point during the interview, you will seem as if you drifted off. When you are working from a list of questions you prepared in advance, remember to eliminate those that were already answered.

Essential

Make a mental note of questions that pop into your head during the interview. You may even come up with questions based on the ones the interviewer asks you. To show you were listening, preface questions that are related to something that was said during the interview with "You mentioned that . . ." or "When you said that . . ."

If you phrase them the right way, your questions can give the interviewer a chance to picture you as her new hire. Instead of asking "What role will *the person you hire* play in the company's plans for expansion," ask "What role will *I* play in the company's plans for expansion." This not only demonstrates your interest in the job, it also encourages the interviewer to consider your qualifications for the job and how you fit into the company's future plans.

Finally, asking questions can show off some of your attributes, namely that you are a good decision-maker and that you are motivated. Both are desirable traits in a new hire. A job candidate who asks intelligent questions demonstrates he is a careful decision-maker who needs to gather information before making a life-changing decision, such as accepting a job offer. Your questions can also serve as proof that you are a motivated person who came to the interview fully prepared. Ask questions that are based on research you did prior to the interview.

Preparing Your Questions

You should prepare a lists of questions in advance and make them specific to each organization with which you are interviewing. First, consider the information you will need in order to decide whether you want to work for this employer. Among the things you might want to know are the company's future plans for growth, its current financial health, rates of employee turnover, and levels of job satisfaction among employees. You probably also want to know what your opportunities for advancement might be.

You are likely to come up with more questions during the interview. As mentioned previously, don't be afraid to ask for clarification of anything you didn't understand. Questions about salary, benefits, and vacation time are off limits at this point. Hold on to those until the employer makes an official job offer.

Questions You *Should* Ask and Questions You *Should Not* Ask

Q Why is this job open?

The answer to this question may help you predict the reception you will receive from current employees if you are hired. If the person you will be replacing left under difficult circumstances, that is, if she was fired or was otherwise forced to leave, her former coworkers may be resentful of anyone who fills her place. You may also learn about the career ladder at this organization. If the previous employee was promoted within the company, you may have a chance for similar advancement down the line.

Q Where would I be working?

This question is a practical one. Pity the person who accepts a job offer only to find out he has to relocate. From your research, you will have learned whether the employer has offices elsewhere. A job advertisement will generally indicate which office has the job opening; if not, this is a fine question to ask.

Q Is there a written job description? May I see it?

You will ask this question simply because you need this information to make an informed decision about whether or not to accept the job.

Q How long have you worked here?

The person interviewing you has a position that is probably several steps above the one for which you are interviewing. Given that fact, the answer to this question will indicate how long it typically takes employees to advance within the company. If the owner of the company is interviewing you, there is no reason to ask this question.

Q What do you like most about your job with this company?

The interviewer is likely one of the few employees of the company with whom you will have contact before you are hired. See what she has to say about working there. The answer to this question, if the interviewer is honest, will weigh in to your decision about accepting a job offer. As with the previous question, ask this only of employees and not the owner of the company.

Alert

Ideally, you should have information about the location and description of a job before the interview, but it may not have been readily available. Be careful, though. If the information was easy to access and you didn't manage to do it, you will look foolish if you ask for it at this late date.

Q In your opinion, what is the best part of this job?

Along the same lines, the answer you receive may help you decide whether the job is right for you. It can also provide you with some valuable insight into the job, especially if your interviewer held the job before being promoted.

Q What is the chain of command?

When you ask questions about the inner workings of a company, it indicates to the employer that you are interested in the job.

Q Who will I be reporting to?

If you find out who your immediate supervisor is, you can try to learn about that person after the interview. Don't forget that you should be gathering information that will help you decide whether to accept an offer if one is made.

Q How many others are in my department?

This will give you a feel for how many people you will work with on a daily basis and what the structure of the group is like. Once again, your prospective employer will be able to note your interest in the position.

Essential

When it comes to asking questions, you should always have some prepared for the interviewer ahead of time. While you may want to write these down for your own reference before the interview, never read directly from this list during the interview.

Q Please describe the corporate culture in this office.

You'll be able to gauge whether this is an environment in which you can see yourself working and being happy.

Q How much interoffice interaction is there? Do departments tend to work independently of one another, or is there a fair amount of intercommunication?

The interviewer will be able to tell you who you'll be working with most often, and if your duties may require you to gain some understanding of other groups within the company.

Q What will I need to do to advance?

Asking this question shows you will be a productive employee who is interested in doing the best job possible. You will do what you need to do to move up.

Q What are my chances for advancement here?

Similar in nature to the previous question, this question shows the employer you are motivated. It also allows you to find out if you will have the opportunity to advance should you work for this employer. That information will help you decide whether to accept a job offer, since you don't want to languish in the same position for a long time.

Q How many people have held this position in the last three years? Why did they leave?

If there is a high rate of turnover in the position for which you are interviewing, you should be suspicious. You should try to find out why this is the case. Is this a difficult employer to work for? Or perhaps the company has expectations that are impossible for employees to meet and they are fired for not meeting them. If you haven't already, access your network to find out if anyone has had any experience with this employer.

Q How long do most employees stay?

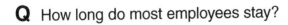

Learning about turnover is a good way to gauge whether employ-ees enjoy working for the employer. A high rate of turnover indicates that most employees aren't satisfied with their jobs, while a low rate of turnover demonstrates a high level of job satisfaction.

Q What reason do most employees give for leaving?

The answer to this question expands on the answer to the prior question. Knowing why employees leave the company helps you find out what you may or may not like about working there. Of course, the interviewer may not know the answer to this question or may not be willing to share it.

 **Question**

What does it mean when an interviewer avoids answering certain questions?
If the interviewer avoids answering reasonable questions—for example, ones about employee turnover—it should send up some red flags for you. What he doesn't say speaks much louder than what he does say. Try to learn more before accepting an offer.

Q How will you decide who to hire?

The answer to this question will let you find out if you missed something during the interview. Was there another skill or qualifica-tion the employer is seeking that you didn't get to talk about? If there was one, try to briefly mention it. If the interviewer seems to be rushing you out the door, it may have to wait. You can use your thank-you let-ter to talk about something that was missed during the interview.

Q When will I hear from you about a decision?

If you know when the employer will make a hiring decision, you won't be left in a state of limbo waiting for the phone to ring. If you don't hear from the employer by a day or two after she says a decision will be made, you can call her. Finally, if you are continuing to interview for other jobs, which you should do until you receive and accept a job offer, you might want to schedule future interviews after the decision date if it's coming up soon.

Q What is the next step? Are you doing second interviews?

This will simply help you know what to expect next.

Q How often are performance evaluations conducted and how are the evaluations made?

You will ask this question to learn what working for this company will be like. You may get a sense of how strict the managers are or how closely the staff is monitored. If you are interviewing for a management position, you will get a sense of how much of your time you will spend on evaluation paperwork.

Q You mentioned something about a training period. How long is it?

This question indicates your interest in the job and shows that you were listening during the interview.

Q Will I have any other opportunities for training?

An employee who inquires about training opportunities is willing to learn as much as possible to do a good job.

Q What types of assignments will I have?

This question indicates you are interested in the job. It also allows you to learn what you will be doing if you are hired.

☀ Alert

Phrase questions in the first, rather than third, person. For example ask "When will I . . ." rather than "When will the person you hire . . ." Doing this will show you are confident and will allow the employer to picture you on the job.

Q How has the company grown over the last five years? Is it profitable?

A company's financial health will help you decide whether to accept a job offer. If the company hasn't grown over the last five years or if it isn't profitable, this should signal that it might not be in the best financial health. Should you accept a job offer, you may be looking for work again soon.

Q What does the company plan to do to keep growing and what role would I play?

The answer to this question will give you information about your prospective employer and the job. You will learn what expectations the employer has for you. By phrasing the question like this, you give the interviewer the chance to picture you in the job for which he is interviewing you.

Q What improvements do you want to make here and how can I help you make them?

Phrasing this question this way allows the employer to envision you as the person she will hire. It will give you a glimpse into the job and the company's plans for the future.

Q In your opinion, how does this company compare to its major competitors, like Activate, Pump, and Dragon Works?

In preparing for the interview you should have researched the prospective employer. When you ask this question, you are saying to the interviewer "Look at the research I've done. I know who your competitors are." The answer to this question will also help you learn more about the company.

Q From my research I learned you sell your products both in the United States and Canada. Do you plan to expand into any other markets?

Again, you are stating something you uncovered in your research. You are also trying to learn something further about the company.

Q I know you sell hair-care products. What are the demographics of your customers?

Your reason for asking this question is similar to your reason for asking the prior one. If you have experience with the demographic this company targets, that is something you can talk about in your thank-you letter or in any follow-up interviews.

Essential

From the interviewer's answer to one of your questions, you discover that one of your skills would be very valuable to the employer's future plans. Bring it up before you leave and again in the thank-you letter you send to follow up on the interview.

Q You mentioned that several of your clients are in the apparel business. What industries are your other clients in?

This question shows you were paying attention during the interview. You also want to learn more about the company's other clients, which demonstrates your interest in the company.

NEVER ASK: How much money will I make?

Money should never be discussed on a job interview. You should hold off on discussing salary until you receive a job offer, when you are in the right position to negotiate. Even if the employer brings it up first, it is best to avoid getting into an extensive conversation about it at this point.

NEVER ASK: What are the health benefits like?

While you may need this information to help you decide whether or not to accept a job offer, the interview isn't the time to obtain it. Hold off on this discussion until you receive a job offer. The person interviewing you may not even know a lot about company benefits other than those she has.

 Fact

Questions about religion are off limits during a job interview. An employer cannot make a decision about whether or not to hire you based on your religion. The earliest you should bring it up or ask for religious observance time is after you've accepted a job offer.

NEVER ASK: How much vacation time will I have?

You haven't even started working and already you want to know about time off? Your goal during the interview is to demonstrate to the employer that you will be a productive employee. Asking about vacation time will not help you reach that goal.

NEVER ASK: Can I take time off for religious observance?

An employer is required by law to give you time off for religious observance, so you have no reason to ask about it during the interview. It should never be brought up during the interview or before you receive a job offer.

NEVER ASK: What does it take to get fired?

Asking this question is kind of like saying, "I want to do as little as possible to get by." Is that how you want the employer to see you?

Chapter 15

What to Do after the Interview

YOU SPENT DAYS, maybe even weeks, getting ready for your job interview. You studied question after question, figuring out how you could best answer each one. You went through your work history to come up with anecdotes that would exemplify your ability to do the job you were being interviewed for. Now the interview is finally over and you think you should feel relieved, but you don't. You haven't been offered the job yet, so all you can do is sit around and wait. Right? Wrong!

Thank-You Letters

The first thing you should do after an interview, aside from sending the interviewer anything he requested, is send a thank-you letter. Job searchers sometimes feel that sending a thank-you letter will make them seem like they are trying to "kiss up" to the interviewer. You don't have any reason to think that, because interviewers rarely see it that way. Sending a thank-you letter is a nice gesture that will let the interviewer know you appreciate the time he spent meeting with you. It will set you apart from other job candidates who choose not to send one.

Who Should Get a Thank-You Letter?

You should send a thank-you letter to each person you met with during your interview. If you met with someone from the human resources department for a screening interview and then met with a department manager, each of them should receive a thank-you note.

If someone showed you around the office, you should send that person a thank-you letter as well. If you had a panel or committee interview, you have to send a thank-you letter to each person who took part in it.

⚡ Alert

Don't send letters addressed as "To Whom It May Concern." Find out the name of each person who interviewed you. If possible, write it down or get that person's business card during the interview. If you didn't get a name, call the receptionist for that information. Make sure you get the correct spelling for each name—spelling counts.

What to Include

The primary purpose of a thank-you letter is to express your gratitude for the time the recipient spent with you. The first thing you should do is say "thank you." Next, take the opportunity to re-emphasize a skill or strength that shows you are the most qualified candidate for the job. If you neglected to mention a particular strength that might help the interviewer make her decision, bring that up in your thank-you letter. If the interviewer voiced concern about something regarding your qualifications, this would be a good time to address that issue.

Finally, you should express your interest in the job. Tell the interviewer you want to work for her. Let her know how she can reach you even if you have already done so. Provide your phone number and an e-mail address if you have one. You want to make it as easy as possible for her to get in touch with you.

Essential

Your thank-you letter should be short and to the point and should never be more than one page long. It should be written using a computer or typewriter, not handwritten. Never address the recipient by first name. Proofread your letter carefully and have someone else look it over too.

E-Mail or Regular Mail?

You may wonder whether to send your thank-you letter by e-mail or by regular mail. The problem with e-mail is that some people don't check theirs on a regular basis. Though it's hard to imagine that this is the case, it is. If you've already corresponded with the employer via e-mail, then it is perfectly okay to send a thank-you e-mail. If you haven't corresponded with her by e-mail and have never been instructed to do so, then send your letter by regular mail.

How to Format a Thank-you Letter

A thank-you letter is considered business correspondence and you must format it accordingly. The format of your letter will differ depending on whether you are sending it by e-mail or by snail mail. In this age of electronic communication, many people have forgotten what a "hard copy" business letter even looks like. Here are the components of a business letter. Add a line after each of the following items:

- **Return address:** Your first and last name (no title) followed by your address should be the first thing on the page.
- **Date:** The date you are sending the letter should appear below the return address, with the name of the month spelled out.

- **Inside address:** The addressee's first and last name (including title, e.g., Mr., Ms., or Dr.), position, company name, and address should appear below the date. Start a new line for each of the following items: name, position, company, street address, and city/town/zip.
- **Salutation:** Your salutation should begin with "Dear" and you should always address the recipient by his title and last name, e.g., Mr. Grey, followed by a colon.
- **Body of letter:** The body of your letter should generally include an introductory paragraph that informs the reader why you are writing to him, one or two paragraphs to give some background or supporting information, and a closing paragraph that wraps everything up and includes information about how the interviewer can reach you.
- **Closing:** End your letter with "Yours truly" or "Sincerely."
- **Signature line:** Skip four or five lines after the closing to leave enough space for your signature, and then type your full name. Don't forget to sign your name after you've printed the letter!

If you are going to send your thank-you letter by e-mail, do not place your return address at the top of the message. Instead you can include that information below your name in the "signature" section of the message. Provide your telephone number or numbers as well. There is no need to include the recipient's address or the date in your message. All e-mail messages are automatically date-stamped.

Sending a thank-you letter by e-mail does not give you an excuse to be any less formal than you would be if you were sending it by regular mail. In the salutation you will address the recipient by title and last name, never by first name. You will word your letter the same way you would have if you sent it by snail mail.

Use your personal e-mail account, not a work e-mail address, to correspond with a potential employer. Do not send the e-mail from anyone's account but your own. If you share an e-mail account with your spouse, you must set up your own account for job search–related use. Use a professional sounding e-mail address, preferably one that includes your name or initials, e.g., *ajones@cablemail.com* is good; *partygirl4eva@cablemail.com* is not.

Alert

Do not use emoticons or e-mail shorthand in your thank-you note. They will make you look unprofessional. Save those things for e-mails you send to your friends. The body of the note should follow the same guidelines as a note sent by regular mail.

Sample Thank-You Letters

Here are four sample thank-you letters. The first three letters are intended for the actual interviewer and the final one is written to an administrative assistant who showed the candidate around the office. The last letter is significantly shorter than the others, and it does not make a point of reiterating any of the writer's skills, since its recipient will not be making the hiring decision and never discussed those skills with the candidate.

Joseph R. Green
14 Willow Street
Hoboken, NJ 07030

June 5, 2009

Ms. Maria Sanchez
Production Manager
Artistic Media
515 Madison Avenue
New York, NY 10022

Dear Ms. Sanchez:

Thank you for meeting with me this afternoon regarding the assistant production manager position at Artistic Media. I appreciate the time you spent getting to know me and explaining the specifics of the job.

I feel strongly that my experience and skills will allow me to make significant contributions to the production team. Artistic Media seems to be a company that values creativity, which is definitely one of my strengths.

I am looking forward to hearing from you within the week, as we discussed. Thank you again for your time and for considering me for this position. You can reach me by phone at (212) 555-4444 or by e-mail at *jgreene@rcat.net.*

Yours truly,

Joe Green

Beverly Smith
1524 South Jefferson Street
Williams, AZ 86046

September 23, 2009

Mr. Connor Shmedley
Customer Service Manager
Smart Mart Stores, Inc.
250 Adams Avenue
Flagstaff, AZ 86001

Dear Mr. Shmedley:

I appreciate your meeting with me this morning regarding the assistant customer service manager job at Smart Mart Stores. I enjoyed having the opportunity to talk to you about the improvements you have planned for the customer service department.

As I mentioned to you during the interview, before I moved to Williams, I worked at Bullseye Stores, which, as you know, has a great reputation for providing customer service. I worked closely with the department manager in implementing many of the procedures that earned Bullseye that reputation. I hope to have the opportunity to work with you to implement such procedures at Smart Mart.

Once again, thank you for taking time out of your busy schedule today. If you have any further questions, you can reach me by phone at (520) 555-5151 or by e-mail at *bevsmith@netco.com*. I look forward to hearing your decision soon.

Sincerely,

Beverly Smith

Sandy Beane
37 Oak Drive
Portland, OR 97205

June 24, 2009

Dr. Pat Lee
26 Tulip Street
Portland, OR 97201

Dear Dr. Lee:

Thank you for taking time out of your busy schedule this afternoon to interview me for the office manager position. I would welcome the opportunity to work with you and the members of your staff.

As you expressed in your interview, you are looking for someone who can manage a very busy office while showing compassion for your patients. Although I have not worked in a medical office, my experience managing a law office has provided me with the skills necessary to do this job well.

Again, thank you for meeting with me. If you have additional questions, you can reach me by phone at (503) 555-1234 or by e-mail at *sbeane@horizon.net*. I look forward to hearing from you regarding your decision.

Yours truly,

Sandy Beane

SAMPLE THANK-YOU LETTER #4

Rose Thornton
105 Peyton Place
Chicago, IL 60637

April 19, 2009

Mr. Richard Rheinhardt
Executive Assistant
Turning Corporation
1543 48th Street
Chicago, IL 60637

Dear Mr. Rheinhardt:

I just wanted to send a quick note to thank you for showing me around your offices on Tuesday after my interview with Janet Parker.

As Ms. Parker mentioned to you, I am interviewing for the book-keeper position. Perhaps we will get to work together.

Yours truly,

Rose Thornton

What to Do If You Don't Want the Job

After the job interview you may decide you would not consider a job offer even if you got one. In that case, you should take yourself out of the running early. While it may be tempting to wait to find out if you got the job, it would not be proper or considerate to do so.

Even if you have decided you don't want the job after all, you should still send a thank-you letter. In that letter, you should thank the recipient for the time she spent meeting with you. You should explain that you no longer want to be considered for the job. If you would like to explain your reasons, go ahead. This is particularly important if you would like to be considered for some other position with the company in the future.

 **Question**

How quickly should I let the employer know I won't consider a job offer?
If you decide you don't want the job on the day of the interview, wait twenty-four hours before you reveal this information to the employer. Give yourself time to change your mind. Once you send that letter, you can't take back your decision.

Here are two sample thank-you letters that let an interviewer know you are no longer interested in the position.

Lisa Evans
4141 Park Road
Evanston, IL 60201

October 3, 2009

Mr. David Grand
Senior Account Executive
Triangle Corporation
314 E. Pine Street
Evanston, IL 60201

Dear Mr. Grand:

Thank you for interviewing me yesterday for the position of assistant account executive. I appreciate the time you spent with me.

After careful consideration I have decided that I am no longer interested in this position.

Again, thank you for your time.

Yours truly,

Lisa Evans

Thomas Jones
75 Bryant Avenue
San Francisco, CA 94108

August 6, 2009

Mr. Eric Peters
Vice President of Product Development
Q & H Corporation
402 West 3rd Street
San Francisco, CA 94108

Dear Mr. Peters:

Thank you for meeting with me yesterday afternoon regarding the marketing assistant position.

After mulling it over for the last twenty-four hours, I would like to take myself out of the running for this position. After spending three years in a similar job, I feel I am now ready for a greater challenge. If a position comes up in which I can better utilize my experience and skills, I hope you'll consider me.

Thank you again for your time. If you have any questions, please call me at (415) 555-2288 or e-mail me at *tjones@homenet.com*.

Sincerely,

Tom Jones

Waiting for a Decision

After the interview, you went home and sent thank-you letters to each person you met with. Now you are sitting around waiting for the phone to ring and checking your e-mail every 5 minutes. Is there anything else you can do to keep yourself from going crazy while you wait to hear something?

What to Do While You Wait

The best thing you can do while waiting to hear from a prospective employer is stick to your usual routine. Doing so will help you stay sane as well as productive. If you are currently employed, your boss probably has no idea you are job hunting. Keep quiet about it even if you are pretty sure you will be offered the job for which you interviewed. Nothing is ever a sure thing until you have an offer in writing. You should also keep your job search campaign active until you receive and accept an offer.

Following Up with the Employer

While there are many situations in your life where it's okay to play hard to get, your job search isn't one of them. There are many reasons you should contact the employer to find out if he has made a decision. There are no reasons not to make the call.

Following up on a job interview is not only your right, it is an important strategy that should be part of your job search campaign. A phone call to a prospective employer shows that you are not someone who is willing to sit around and wait quietly while someone else makes a decision about your future. It also gives you another opportunity to sell yourself to the employer if you find out he hasn't yet made a decision.

You may be hesitant to call an employer to find out if he has made a hiring decision because you don't want to look anxious or pushy. As long as you go about it in the right way, you won't. You should call the employer exactly one week after the interview, unless the interviewer told you he would be making a decision by a certain date. In that case, call a day after that date.

Call the person who has been your contact at the prospective employer's company. Politely, but not meekly, ask if they have made a decision yet. If they haven't, ask when they expect to make one.

⚡ Alert

Don't make a pest of yourself by calling your prospective employer too often. If the employer tells you she will make a decision in a week, don't call back before then. As a general rule, don't call more than once a week. You don't want the act of finding out whether you got the job to cost you the job.

The Job Offer—Finally

So, you have a job offer. Congratulations! By this time it's likely that you've decided whether you want to work for the company. Of course, you will have to consider the offer they made and decide whether to accept it.

Negotiating a Job Offer

Some job candidates feel negotiating an offer is a must, regardless of what that offer is. Others would not even consider negotiating and accept the offer as is. The truth is, there is no right way to go. It all depends on the offer. It is up to you to determine whether the offer the employer made is fair. If it isn't, you have to decide whether you want to negotiate for a better one.

If you decide to negotiate for a better offer, be sure to do your homework first. Find out how much others working in your field earn. Talk to people working in your field. Look at salary surveys. Ask other employers. Consult your trade or professional association.

Question

Is it always possible to negotiate a job offer?
You can't always negotiate a job offer. Sometimes salary and benefits are set through a contractual arrangement between a union and an employer. If only the salary is set through such an arrangement, you may be able to negotiate other benefits, such as the amount of vacation time you will receive

Salaries are often reported as a range. Don't compare oranges and tangerines. Candidates with more experience, greater educational levels, and better skills will lean toward the higher end of that range. You should also be aware that salaries differ depending on where a job is located. Depending on regional variances in cost of living or in demand for certain skill sets, salaries can be higher in certain parts of the country. They can also vary according to your proximity to a large metropolitan area. If you get extensive benefits, such as health insurance, your monetary salary may be lower than it would be if that was not included in your offer.

A job offer isn't official until you see it in black and white. Do not give notice to your current employer until you have a written offer from your future employer. You should, in turn, send a written acceptance of the job offer. If you decide to decline the offer, it is polite to send the employer a letter to inform him of that. Good luck with your new job!

Appendix A

Resources

Websites

The Internet is a great place to turn to for career-related information. You can get career and job search advice; find job listings; and research occupations, salaries, and prospective employers.

Career and Job Search Advice Websites

About.com Career Planning
The Everything® Practice Interview Book, 2nd Edition author Dawn Rosenberg McKay's site covers all aspects of career planning including career choice, job hunting, job training, legal issues, and the workplace.
http://careerplanning.about.com

About.com Job Searching
Alison Doyle, the guide to this excellent site, helps you with all aspects of online job searching, writing resumes and cover letters, references, interviewing skills, and unemployment.
http://jobsearch.about.com

About.com Human Resources
Get the employer's perspective from Susan M. Heathfield, the guide to this comprehensive site. .
http://humanresources.about.com

Career Journal

Career Journal is the *Wall Street Journal's* career site and is geared toward executives, managers, and professionals. It includes salary and hiring information, job search advice, and career management help. There is also a searchable database of jobs in select fields.
www.careerjournal.com

JobHuntersBible

Dick Bolles runs this site as a supplement to his well-known book *What Color Is Your Parachute?* He has included a variety of tools, including career and personality tests and advice that will help you with your career and job search.
www.jobhuntersbible.com

Monster Career Advice

Find resume and job interviewing tips, salary information, relocating advice, and diversity advice from Monster.com.
http://content.monster.com

Riley Guide

Librarian Margaret F. Dikel has organized myriad sites that can help you with your job search.
www.rileyguide.com

Online Job Banks

CareerBuilder.com

Through its partnerships with several major newspaper publishers, CareerBuilder.com lists local jobs from newspaper help wanted sections from around the country. Search this huge jobs database by location, company, job type, and industry. You can even search in Spanish.
www.careerbuilder.com

CollegeGrad.com

This job board specifically targets college graduates and recent graduates who are looking for entry-level jobs.
www.collegegrad.com

FlipDog
FlipDog collects job announcements from company websites. Search for jobs by employer, keyword, and category or post your resume.
www.flipdog.com

govtjobs.com
Search for jobs with states, counties, towns, and cities.
www.govtjobs.com

Indeed
Indeed is a job search engine. When you put in your search criteria, it looks through many different sites including job boards, corporate websites, professional association websites, and newspapers.
www.indeed.com

Jobster
Jobster compiles job listings from around the Internet, but employers can also post open positions directly to this site. You can network with other Jobster members.
www.jobster.com

Monster
Search for jobs by location or job category. You can also enter keywords to search by job titles, company names, and requirements. Post your resume online so employers can find you. If you sign up for a newsfeed, you will receive updates on jobs that meet criteria you specify.
www.monster.com

SimplyHired
Go to this site to find job listings gathered from company websites, classified ads, and job boards.
www.simplyhired.com

USAJOBS

This is the official site of the U.S. Office of Personnel Management. You can search for jobs with the federal government, create a resume, and download related forms.
www.usajobs.com

Yahoo! HotJobs

Search for a job by keyword, job category, or location. You can post your resume and let employers find you. You can even block certain employers from seeing your resume.
http://hotjobs.yahoo.com

Company Research Resources and Tools

Bloglines

A web-based newsfeed reader that allows you to subscribe to and read newsfeeds and blogs.
www.bloglines.com

Fortune 500 Business Blogging Wiki

Look here for blogs maintained by employees of *Fortune* 500 companies.
www.socialtext.net/bizblogs/index.cgi

Google Blog Search

Locate blogs about the industries and companies you are researching.
http://blogsearch.google.com

Google Reader

A web-based newsfeed reader. Use it to subscribe to blogs and newsfeeds.
www.google.com/reader

MySpace: Company/Coworker Groups
Many company and coworker groups have MySpace pages. You can
search for the one in which you are interested by choosing "Groups"
under the "More" dropdown list, and then "Companies/Coworkers."
Many are public, which means you can access them. Don't post if
you don't work there.
www.myspace.com

PR Newswire
Use this site to search for press releases put out by various
companies.
www.prnewswire.com

Security and Exchange Commission Filings and Forms (EDGAR)
The Securities and Exchange Commission requires publicly held
companies to file information about finances each quarter and
information about material events or corporate changes as they
occur. You can retrieve this information from the EDGAR database.
www.sec.gov/edgar.shtml

Technorati Blog Search
Use this site to search for blogs that cover a particular industry or
company. You can also search for individual blog posts by topic.
http://technorati.com

Topix
Search for news about companies and industries.
www.topix.com

Occupation and Salary Information

JobStar Profession-Specific Salary Surveys
Look here for salary information for dozens of occupations.
www.jobstar.org/tools/salary/sal-prof.cfm

Job Futures
This resource contains descriptions of occupations and labor market information. It is produced by the Canadian government. Find information for all of Canada or for individual provinces.
www.jobfutures.ca

Occupational Outlook Handbook
Use this resource, published by the U.S. Bureau of Labor Statistics and updated biannually, to get job descriptions. Learn about working conditions, training and education needed, employment outlook, salary, and expected job prospects for a wide number of occupations.
www.bls.gov/oco/home.htm

Salary.com
Get salary information for a variety of occupations.
www.salary.com

Career Networking

Facebook
Although it is usually used by high school and college students for social networking, Facebook can also be used to network with other professionals.
www.facebook.com

LinkedIn
Use this online network to connect with other professionals, search for jobs, and get found by potential employers.
www.linkedin.com

Miscellaneous Sites

Action Words from Purdue University's Online Writing Lab
Are you looking for just the right word to describe your skills and accomplishments? You will find it here, arranged into categories.
http://owl.english.purdue.edu/owl/resource/543/02

Equal Employment Opportunity Commission
This government agency was established by the Civil Rights Act of 1964 and protects U.S. workers from many types of employment discrimination. The EEOC website has information on all the laws the agency enforces and advice on how to file a claim.
www.eeoc.gov

ExecutivePlanet.com
This website includes business culture guides for international businesspeople.
www.executiveplanet.com

Books

Job Search Advice

Bolles, Richard Nelson, and Dale S. Brown. *Job-Hunting for the So-Called Handicapped or People Who Have Disabilities.* Berkeley, CA: Ten Speed Press, 2000.

Bolles, Richard Nelson. *What Color Is Your Parachute: A Practical Manual for Job-Hunters and Career-Changers.* Berkeley, CA: Ten Speed Press, Annual.

McKay, Dawn Rosenberg. *The Everything® Get-a-Job Book, 2nd Edition.* Avon, MA: Adams Media, 2007.

Wendleton, Kate. *Kick off Your Career: Write a Winning Resume, Ace Your Interview, Negotiate a Great Salary.* Clifton Park, NY: Cengage Delmar Learning, 2002.

Yate, Martin. *Knock 'em Dead: The Ultimate Job Search Guide.* Avon, MA: Adams Media, Annual.

Career Advancement

Covey, Stephen R. *The 7 Habits of Highly Effective People.* New York: Free Press, 2004.

Darling, Diane. *The Networking Survival Guide: Get the Success You Want by Tapping into the People You Know.* New York: McGraw-Hill, 2003.

Johnson, Tori, and Robyn Freedman Spizman. *Take This Book to Work.* New York: St. Martin's Press, 2006.

Cover Letters and Resumes

Enelow, Wendy S., and Louise M. Kursmark. *Expert Resumes for Computer and Web Jobs.* St. Paul, MN: JIST Publishing, 2005.

———. *Expert Resumes for Health Care Careers.* St. Paul, MN: JIST Publishing, 2003.

———. *Expert Resumes for People Returning to Work.* St. Paul, MN: JIST Publishing, 2008.

Kursmark, Louise M. *Best Resumes for College Students and New Grads.* St. Paul, MN: JIST Publishing, 2005.

Nadler, Burton Jay. *The Everything® Cover Letter Book, 2nd Edition.* Avon, MA: Adams Media, 2005.

Noble, David F. *Gallery of Best Resumes for People Without a Four-Year Degree.* St. Paul, MN: JIST Publishing, 2004.

Parker, Yana. *The Damn Good Resume Guide: A Crash Course in Resume Writing.* Berkeley, CA: Ten Speed Press, 2002.

Parker, Yana. *The Resume Catalog: 200 Damn Good Examples.* Berkeley, CA: Ten Speed Press, 1996.

Provenzano, Steven. *Blue Collar Resumes.* Clifton Park, NY: Delmar Cengage Learning, 1999.

Wallace, Richard. *Adams Cover Letter Almanac, 2nd Edition.* Avon, MA: Adams Media, 2006.

———. *Adams Resume Almanac, 2nd Edition.* Avon, MA: Adams Media, 2005.

Yate, Martin. *Knock 'em Dead Cover Letters.* Avon, MA: Adams Media, 2008.

Yate, Martin. *Knock 'em Dead Resumes.* Avon, MA: Adams Media, 2008.

Interview Etiquette and Style

Gross, Kim Johnson, and Jeff Stone. *Chic Simple Dress Smart for Men: Wardrobes That Win in the New Workplace.* New York: Grand Central Publishing, 2002.

————. *Chic Simple Dress Smart for Women: Wardrobes That Win in the New Workplace.* New York: Grand Central Publishing, 2002.

Post, Emily, and Peter Post. *Emily Post's The Etiquette Advantage in Business.* New York: HarperCollins, 2005.

Sabath, Ann Marie. *Business Etiquette: 101 Ways to Conduct Business with Charm and Savvy.* New York: Fall River Press, 2006.

International Job Searching

Axtell, Roger E. *Essential Do's and Taboos: The Complete Guide to International Business and Leisure Travel.* Hoboken, NJ: John Wiley & Sons, 2007.

Krannich, Ronald L., and Wendy S. Enelow. *Best Resumes and CVs for International Jobs: Your Passport to the Global Job Market.* Manassas Park, VA: Impact Publications, 2002.

Morrison, Terri. *Kiss, Bow, or Shake Hands, 2nd Edition: The Best-selling Guide to Doing Business in More Than 60 Countries.* Avon, MA: Adams Media, 2006.

Salary Negotiation

Chapman, Jack. *Negotiating Your Salary: How to Make $1000 a Minute.* Berkeley, CA: Ten Speed Press, 2005.

Pinkley, Robin L., and Gregory B. Northcraft. *Get Paid What You're Worth: The Expert Negotiators' Guide to Salary and Compensation.* New York: St. Martin's Press, 2003.

Appendix B

Glossary

acceptance letter
A letter informing an employer of one's decision to accept a job offer.

accomplishment
Something at which you succeeded as a direct result of your efforts.

achievement
See *accomplishment*.

Americans with Disabilities Act (ADA)
A federal civil rights law that was designed to prevent discrimination and enable those with disabilities to participate fully in all aspects of society.

annual report
The primary document public companies use to disclose corporate information to shareholders.

background check
Used by prospective employers to verify the information included on a job candidate's resume or application, including work history and educational background; may also include looking at criminal records and credit history.

behavioral interview
An interview during which the interviewer asks the job candidate to demonstrate her competencies by giving real-life examples of when she has used those competencies. This may be either a standalone entity or part of a regular job interview.

benefits
The part of your compensation package that is in addition to salary. May include health and life insurance, personal days, vacation, pension plans, tuition assistance, and severance packages.

body language
The nonverbal gestures and mannerisms used to interpret one's true feelings.

career coach
A career development expert who advises clients about job searching and career advancement.

career counselor
A career development expert who usually has a master's degree in counseling and often is licensed by a state board of licensure.

career exploration
This step of the career planning process involves gathering information about an occupation in order to make a decision regarding career choice.

Certified Professional Resume Writer (CPRW)
A resume writer who is certified by the Professional Association of Resume Writers.

chronological resume
A resume on which work experience is listed in reverse chronological order (that is, the most recent job is at the top of the list).

Civil Rights Act of 1964, Title VII
This federal law prohibits employment discrimination based on an individual's race, religion, sex, or national origin.

civil service
Employment in the federal government, or in a state or local government.

combination resume
A resume that combines the information included on both a functional and a chronological resume; skills are emphasized but an employment history is included.

committee interview
See *panel interview.*

competencies
A combination of your knowledge, skills, and abilities.

confidentiality agreement
Part of an employment contract that prohibits an employee from disclosing confidential or sensitive information; also referred to as a *nondisclosure agreement.*

corporate culture
The shared values, goals, and practices that give a corporation its unique personality.

cover letter
A letter sent along with a resume; the cover letter's purpose is to introduce the job seeker to the person who will be reviewing the resume and to express the candidate's interest in the job.

curriculum vitae (CV)
A summary of one's work experience that is much more detailed than a resume; it includes academic background, publications, and other professional achievements.

Equal Employment Opportunity Commission (EEOC)
The federal agency that oversees the enforcement of antidiscrimination laws.

exempt employee
Refers to employees who are exempt from the overtime and minimum wage provisions of the Fair Labor Standards Act; exempt employees are generally those working in executive, administrative, professional, or outside sales positions.

Fair Labor Standards Act (FLSA)
U.S. law that establishes minimum wage, overtime pay, record-keeping, and child labor standards; these standards affect nonexempt full-time and part-time employees in the private sector as well as in federal, state, and local governments.

Family and Medical Leave Act (FLMA)
Enacted in 1993, this federal law allows for a leave from work for the birth or adoption of a child or one's own illness or that of a family member.

Form 10-Q
A quarterly report that a publicly held company files with the SEC.

Form 8-K
The form a publicly held company must file with the SEC to report the occurrence of any material events or corporate changes.

functional resume
A resume on which skills are categorized by job function; abilities are emphasized rather than work history.

glass ceiling
A term that refers to the invisible barrier which certain groups, e.g., women and minorities, cannot pass to reach higher career levels.

goal, long-term:
A career or personal objective that can take from three to five years to complete.

goal, short-term
A career or personal objective that can be reached in one to three years.

group interview
A job interview during which a group of candidates are interviewed at the same time.

hard skills
The skills you learned in school or through some other formal training.

hiring manager
The person for whom a job candidate will work if hired; the hiring manager interviews and selects the candidate.

human resources (HR) department
The department in a company that is responsible for selection, hiring, and training employees; sometimes referred to as the *personnel department.*

illegal questions
Technically, the questions that a prospective employer cannot, by law, ask a job candidate. Often refers to questions used to gather information which the employer cannot use to make a hiring decision because of antidiscrimination laws. See also *Equal Employment Opportunity Commission.*

informational interview
A meeting during which someone planning his or her career learns about an occupation from someone who has firsthand knowledge.

internship
A work experience, usually unpaid and often done for academic credit, that is usually related to one's field of study.

interpersonal skills
One's ability to get along with others.

job banks
Websites that list job openings and allow users to search through them by location, job type, and often keywords such as job title and employer. See also *resume banks.*

job club
A group of people who meet to offer support to one another during the job search process; usually help is offered in resume writing, job interviewing, and networking.

job description
Provides details about a job, such as duties, requirements, and hours.

job objective
The section of a resume that tells a prospective employer what type of job the candidate is seeking.

job offer
An offer made to a job candidate by the prospective employer; a job offer usually includes specifics about the job, such as salary, benefits, hours, and starting date.

job posting
A notice announcing that a job is available; it usually gives some details about the position and its requirements.

job reference
Someone the potential employer may contact to ask about a job candidate; generally this person will be able to recommend that the employer hire this person.

job reference list
A neatly formatted list of job references that includes names and contact information.

mentor
One who provides guidance for a less-experienced colleague.

mock job interview
A practice job interview that is sometimes videotaped.

network
The group of individuals with whom one can share career-related information.

noncompete agreement
Part of an employment contract or a separate agreement that states one will not compete with his or her employer; an employee may be asked to sign a noncompete agreement upon being hired; also referred to as a *noncompete clause*.

nondisclosure agreement
See *confidentiality agreement*.

nonexempt employee
Refers to employees who are covered by the Fair Labor Standards Act; nonexempt employees must receive overtime pay and must be paid at least the current minimum wage.

panel interview
A job interview during which a group of people interview a job candidate; also referred to as a *committee interview*.

personality inventory
A tool used to find out what personality type one fits into; personality inventories are used as self-assessment tools.

portfolio
A collection of work; a portfolio generally contains pictures, photographs, or writing samples, but may include any work samples a job candidate wants a prospective employer to see.

Pregnancy Discrimination Act of 1978
An amendment to Title VII of the Civil Rights Act of 1964 that protects a woman from being discriminated against based on her pregnancy or related condition.

privately held company
A company owned by individuals or groups of individuals.

publicly held company
A company that has shares of stock that are traded on a stock exchange. The owners of the shares of stock are called shareholders and they have a financial stake in the company.

qualifications
The knowledge, skills, and abilities a job candidate must have in order to be hired for a particular position.

reasonable accommodation
Adjustments or modifications to the workplace provided by an employer to enable people with disabilities to enjoy equal employment opportunities.

reference
See *job reference.*

rejection letter
A letter informing an employer of one's decision to reject a job offer.

resume
A summary of one's work history and educational background; a resume is usually one page in length; see also *chronological resume, combination resume,* and *functional resume.*

resume banks
Websites that allow users to post resumes so employers may search through them to find eligible applicants.

salary history
A document included as an addendum to the resume; lists salaries for each job on the resume.

salary negotiation
The process a job candidate goes through to obtain the best possible compensation package.

screening interview
The initial interview with a prospective employer. Usually someone from the human resources department will try to verify items on the candidate's resume, such as dates of employment, schooling, etc.

Securities and Exchange Commission (SEC)
The U.S. government agency that protects investors and maintains the integrity of the securities market.

selection interview
The interview during which the hiring manager will try to determine if the applicant is the best-qualified job candidate.

sexual harassment
Unwelcome sexual advances, requests for sexual favors, or other verbal or physical conduct of a sexual nature; rejection of this conduct may have a negative effect on one's employment, work performance, or create an intimidating, hostile, or offensive work environment; sexual harassment violates the Civil Rights Act of 1964.

soft skills
Skills that aren't specific to any occupation, but instead enhance one's performance regardless of what one's actual job is.

stress interview
A technique sometimes used by interviewers to weed out job candidates who can't handle adversity; the interviewer purposely makes the candidate uncomfortable or anxious.

thank-you letter
A letter a job candidate should send, following a job interview, to each person who participated in his interview.

transferable skills
Skills one has gathered through jobs, hobbies, volunteer work, or other life experiences that can be used in future jobs or in a new career.

work history
Past jobs as described on one's resume.

vita
See *curriculum vitae.*

Index

A

Abilities, 57–74
Accomplishments, 7, 75–92,
   156, 220, 242
Advancement opportunities, 250
Age discrimination, 204, 207
Antidiscrimination laws, 202, 205
Anxiety, 18–19, 32
Asking for job, 35–36
Asking questions, 244–56
Attire, 22–27, 169
Auditing skills, 66–67
Awards, 82–83

B

Behavioral interviews, 222–43
Benefits, 255
"Big fish," 162
Birthplace, 203, 208
Body language, 31–34, 209
Books, 278–80
Bosses, 115–17, 135, 186. *See also*
   Managers; Supervisors
Briefcase, 27
Budget-writing, 177

C

Career choices, 56, 200–201
Career goals, 45, 50–51, 77,
   81–82, 87, 155, 237
Career journal, 76
Career path deviations, 61, 119–20
Career preference, 151–52
Career progression, 78–81,
   124, 189, 195–96
Careers, changing, 61
Career success, 78–81
Chain of command, 248–49
Challenges, accepting, 171–73
Change, adapting to, 50
Child-care arrangements, 212–13
Children, 211–12
Client knowledge, 157, 161
Clients, handling, 173–74, 180–81, 243
College assignments, 106
College grades, 107, 108
College jobs, 115
College preparation, 104–9
College questions, 53–54,
   93–110, 115, 192
College transfers, 104

Command, chain of, 248–49
Communication skills, 17, 61, 68–69
Company, contributing
   to, 150–51, 165–66
Company, researching, 7–16, 147–64
Company competitors, 161
Company data, 149–53, 254–55
Company directories, 12
Company expectations, 166–67
Company goals, 154, 237
Company growth, 253–54
Company mission, 163
Company news, 12–16
Company preference, 150–51
Company questions, 246–55
Complaints, handling, 67
Computer skills, 64–65, 70–71
Confidence, 19–20, 209
Conflicts, resolving, 129–31, 232–33
Contributing to company,
   150–51, 165–66
Convictions, 191, 215–16
Corporate culture, 24, 169, 249
Coworkers, 49–50, 137–40,
   233–35, 249–50
Crimes, 191, 215–16
Crisis, handling, 62–63
Criticism, handling, 144
Current job, 113–15, 118, 121–23, 162
Customer service, 70–71,
   142–43, 172, 234–35

D

Dating, 140–41
Decision, waiting on, 269–70
Decision-making skills, 52, 121,
   179, 223, 230–36, 240–41
Declining job offer, 266–68

Delegating skills, 48–49, 62,
   230–31, 239, 241
Difficult questions, 183–201
Dinner interviews, 36–38
Directions, following, 67
Disabilities, 204–5, 216–17
Disagreements, 61, 132
Discrimination, 67, 160, 202–10
Dress code, 24, 169
Dressing for interviews, 22–27
Drug use, 218–19

E

Education questions, 93–110, 199.
   See also College questions
Electives, 105
Embarrassing questions, 183–201
Emergency notification, 220
Employee expectations, 165–82
Employee issues, 134, 140–46,
   158–59, 163, 168, 174, 232–33.
   See also Supervisor skills
Employee turnover, 72, 77, 250–51
Employer, researching, 7–16, 147–64
Employers, 115–17, 135, 186
Employment gaps, 184,
   187–91, 198–200
Evaluating others, 134
Evaluation of perfor-
   mance, 136–37, 252
Exiting interview, 35–36
Expectations, 165–82
Extracurricular activities, 99
Eye contact, 33

F

Facebook, 200–201
Fact-finding skills, 239–40

Failure, handling, 44, 92
Family, 211–12, 214, 219
Favorite boss, 115–16
Favorite jobs, 113
Favorite subjects, 98, 102–3
Felonies, 191, 216
Fields, changing, 61, 119–20
Figures, presenting, 239
Fingernails, 25
Firings, 184–85, 188, 243, 256
First impressions, 22–39
First job, 113
Flexibility, 230
Follow-up, 269–70
Foreign countries, 38–39
Fundraising skills, 70, 197

G
GED, 199
Gender identity, 210
Glossary, 281–87
Goals, 45, 50–51, 77, 81–82,
    87, 154–55, 237
GPAs, 107
Group therapy skills, 69

H
Hairstyle, 25
Handbags/purses, 27
Handshake, 34
Hard skills, 57–58
Hard work, 53
Health benefits, 255
Health questions, 204–5, 216–19
Height questions, 210
High school, 107–8, 199. *See
    also* Education questions

Hiring procedure, 251–52
Hiring questions, 165–82
Hobbies, 52

I
Ideal company, 158
Ideal coworker, 137
Ideal employee, 138
Ideal job, 157–58
Ideal manager, 137–38
Ideal work environment, 55
Illegal drug use, 218
Illegal questions, 202–21
Internet searches, 200–201
Internships, 100–101
Interpersonal skills, 128–46,
    224–27, 233–36
Interview, beginning, 29–31
Interview, following, 257–71
Interview, rehearsing, 16–17, 31
Interview, understanding, 1–5
Interview preparations, 1–21
Interview process, 2–3
Interview purpose, ix–x
Interview tips, viii
Interview types, 4–5

J
Job, asking for, 35–36
Job, declining, 266–68
Job considerations, 125–26
Job description, 10, 58,
    62, 133, 247, 248
Job dissatisfaction, 143–44
Job duties, 123–24, 154–58
Job history, 111–27
Job offer, 269–71

Job preference, 151–52
Jobs, choosing, 121–22
Jobs, fired from, 184–85, 188, 256
Jobs, learning from, 117–19
Jobs, leaving, 122–23,
   126–27, 184–88, 194
Juggling projects, 65–66

K

Knowledge, proving, 147–49

L

Leadership skills, 43–44,
   47–48, 99, 100, 237
Learning skills, 74
Listening skills, 67
Lying, 7, 54, 76, 184, 191,
   193, 215, 218, 240

M

Majors, 95–97, 103–4, 194
Make-up, 25
Managerial skills, 60, 71, 138, 140, 243
Managers, 120, 137–38
Marital status, 204, 212–15
Market, understanding, 170
MBAs, 104
Mealtime interviews, 36–38
Medical office skills, 73
Meeting interviewer, 30
Mental health questions, 217–18
Military experience, 62
"Million-dollar" winnings, 55–56
Motivation, 87–88, 225
Multitasking skills, 223, 230–32
MySpace, 200–201

N

Nails, 25
National origin, 203, 208–9
Networking, 17–18
Nursing skills, 73

O

Obstacles, overcoming, 86–87, 91–92
On-call situations, 166, 179–80
Organizational skills, 61, 66, 74, 97,
   100, 223, 227, 229, 231–32, 241
Overqualified status, 190–92

P

Parental status, 204, 211–12
Performance evalua-
   tions, 136–37, 252
Personal goals, 77, 81–82
Personality, revealing, 40–56, 128–46
Personality conflicts, 129–32
Personal questions, 40–56, 207–10
Persuasion skills, 141, 197, 238, 242
Pet peeves, 49–50
Policy disagreements, 135–36
Political affiliation, 204, 214
Portfolio, 27
Position, defining, 159
Posture, 33–34
Pregnancy, 204
Presentation skills, 60,
   226, 238, 241–42
Present job, 113–15, 118, 121–23, 162
Pressure, handling, 48–49
Prioritizing, 63, 65–66
Problem-solving skills, 63–64, 89–90,
   141–46, 223, 229, 231, 236–40, 243
Product development, 163–64, 175

Professional goals, 45, 50–51, 77, 81–82, 87, 155, 237
Professional reading, 51
Professors, 104, 105
Program director skills, 71–72
Projects, juggling, 65–66
Promotions, 78–81, 84, 88, 124
Promptness, 28–29
Purses/handbags, 27

Q

Questions, answering, 4
Questions, asking, 244–56
Questions, avoid asking, viii, 255–56
Questions, understanding, 169

R

Race, 203, 208
Reading materials, 51
Real-life experiences, 143, 228
Recent graduates, 80, 93–94
Reconsidering job, 266–68
Rehearsing interviews, 16–17, 31
Religion, 160, 180, 203–4, 210–11, 255
Relocating, 160, 181, 197–98
Researching compa-
    nies, 7–16, 147–64
Research skills, 71, 125–26,
    231–32, 239–40
Resources, 272–80
Responsibility, 125, 190
Resume, copies of, 27
Resume, studying, 5–7, 112
Rewards, 82–83, 88–89
Risk-taking, 47

S

Salary, 127, 182, 255, 270–71
Sales skills, 69, 197
Samples of work, 27
School, 53–55, 107–8, 199. See
    also Education questions
Second interviews, 4, 23, 252
Self-confidence, 19–20, 209
Sexual orientation, 204, 210, 219–21
Shaking hands, 34
Shoes, 26–27
Siblings, 46–47
Skills, acquiring, 64
Skills, discussing, 57–74, 147–49
Skills, using, 57–59
Soft skills, 58–59
Software skills, 64–65, 70–71
Staff, handling, 134, 168, 174. See
    also Employee issues
Strengths, 46
Stress, handling, 48–49, 178–79
Stress, and interviews, 18–19, 32
Subordinates, 131, 186–87
Success, handling, 44, 78–81, 88
Success, traits for, 74, 149–50
Suits, 22–23
Supervisors, 120–21, 131–34,
    189, 193, 249
Supervisor skills, 72, 74, 124, 132,
    134, 143, 168, 176–77. See
    also Employee issues

T

Tardiness, 28
Tax returns, handling, 65
Teacher influences, 96–97
Teaching skills, 68–69

Team-building skills, 224, 228, 237
Teamwork, 45–46, 74,
    83–84, 172–73, 227
Thank-you letters, 255, 257–65
Therapy skills, 69
Time-management skills, 63,
    74, 223, 226–27, 229, 232
Training period, 252–53
Training skills, 170–71
Travel, 125, 166–67, 174–75,
    177–78, 199, 219
Trust, 176–77
Typical day at work, 114

Working alone, 42–43, 45–46
Working independently, 46,
    132, 168, 172–73, 234
Working late, 166–67, 176, 180
Working long hours, 166, 169, 214
Workplace violence, 130
Work samples, 27
Writing skills, 99, 224, 232

U

Under-qualified status, 195–96
Unhappy customers, 142–43. See
    also Customer service
Union affiliation, 205–6, 213
University questions, 53–54,
    93–110, 115, 192

V

Vacation time, 255
Value to company, 82–83
Videotape interviews, 17, 31
Violence, 130

W

Weaknesses, 43–44
Websites, 272–78
Weight questions, 207–8
Work environment, 55
Work experience, lack of,
    80, 93–94, 194–95
Work history, 111–27